Borrowing Inequality

Borrowing Inequality

Race, Class, and Student Loans

Derek V. Price

LYNNE
RIENNER
PUBLISHERS

BOULDER
LONDON

Published in the United States of America in 2004 by
Lynne Rienner Publishers, Inc.
1800 30th Street, Boulder, Colorado 80301
www.rienner.com

and in the United Kingdom by
Lynne Rienner Publishers, Inc.
3 Henrietta Street, Covent Garden, London WC2E 8LU

Library of Congress Cataloging-in-Publication Data
Price, Derek V.
    Borrowing inequality : race, class, and student loans / Derek V. Price
      p. cm.
    Includes bibliographical references and index.
    ISBN 1-58826-216-2 (alk. paper)
    1. Student loan funds—United States.   2. Discrimination in higher education—
United States. I. Title.
LB2340.P75   2004
378.3'62—dc22

                                        2003058571

British Cataloguing in Publication Data
A Cataloguing in Publication record for this book
is available from the British Library.

Printed and bound in the United States of America

5   4   3   2   1

Contents

Tables and Figures

Tables

Figures

Acknowledgments

A s with any project, several organizations and individuals contributed support, advice, and encouragement. First, my thanks to Robert C. Dickeson, whose support for independent inquiry into postsecondary access and success made this book possible. Thanks also to the American Educational Research Association's "AERA Grants Program," which supported portions of this project under NSF grant #RED-9980573. This program receives funds from the U.S. Department of Education's National Center for Education Statistics and the National Science Foundation. I also thank the National Center for Public Policy and Higher Education (especially Pat Callan and Joni Finney) and my fellow national associates, whose commitment to expanding postsecondary opportunities is beyond dispute. The ideas and opinions in this book do not necessarily represent the views of these organizations, their staff, officers, or boards of directors.

I am especially grateful to Jerry Sheehan Davis, who recruited me into the domain of higher education policy analysis and who continues to encourage my idealist tendencies while pointing out the boundaries of political realities. Similarly, Fred Galloway is my mentor in research design, and his thoughtful advice makes me a better social scientist.

Several researchers and policy analysts read various drafts of this book or engaged me in stimulating debate and conversation. In particular, Jill Wohlford, Scott Thomas, Catherine Millet, Laura Perna, Jamie Merisotis, Ken Redd, Colleen O'Brien, Ed St. John, and Brian Pusser provided insightful and knowledgeable guidance. In addition, three anonymous reviewers provided important feedback during the manuscript review process. A special thanks to my close friend and scholar, Dave Ramsaran, who provided an oasis for my research and writing during the predictable blocks that accompanied my work.

My editors at Lynne Rienner Publishers, Bridget Julian and Alan McClare, also have my gratitude. Bridget pursued this project when I was an assistant professor at Morehead State University and stuck with me during the inevitable delays that accompanied my transition from academe to private philanthropy. Alan entered midstream and pushed me along to completion, reminding me of agreed-upon deadlines and the production schedule.

Finally, I could not have completed this book without the love and support of my wife, Lori. She put up with my self-absorption throughout this project, and she spent hours helping my words articulate the ideas in my head. I dedicate this book to our children, Madeline and Benjamin, through whose eyes I see the potential for a new world where all people live in peace and justice, and through whose spirit I continue to dream.

Of course, I take full responsibility for the ideas and opinions expressed herein, and any omissions or errors are my own.

Borrowing Inequality

Introduction

During the last two decades of the twentieth century, the transition to an information economy developed alongside the export of well-paid manufacturing jobs to low-wage havens in developing countries. The old economy manufacturing jobs that did not require a degree beyond high school and provided a middle-class lifestyle are becoming a smaller share of the occupational structure of the U.S. economy. Technological advances and the rapid exchange of knowledge and information that require a workforce with advanced educational credentials drive the economic opportunities in the twenty-first century. According to the U.S. Department of Labor, 42 percent of the job growth in the first decade of this information century will require some form of postsecondary credential.

These trends in economic development are functions of global economic "integration" and enhance the power of higher education as an arbiter of socioeconomic opportunities within the United States. Indeed, higher education controls the allocation of educational credentials, which are becoming more central to determining access to jobs, goods, and economic security. Higher education also provides social benefits: a more educated citizenry increases economic productivity, enhances the quality of life among diverse communities, and strengthens democratic political institutions. As the college credential replaces the high school diploma as the required level of educational competency, expanding access to higher education should be a priority of public policy. Yet higher education is not available universally or subsidized adequately so as to be within reach of all qualified students. On the contrary, persons from low-income backgrounds and race and ethnic minorities do not experience equal opportunity for higher education compared to upper-income students and more affluent whites. This educational inequity undermines the long-term economic prosperity of the nation, threatens democratic institutions by weakening civic participation, and undermines the ability of the United States to maintain its leadership among the world's nations.

The U.S. higher education system operates with the support and encouragement of federal and state governments. After World War II, politicians, communities, and corporations expressed nearly universal support for education as a national priority. Between the 1940s and 1970s, the federal government made considerable investments in the human resources of U.S. citizens through the GI Bill and Basic Educational Opportunity Grants (later known as Pell Grants). The widespread consensus about the importance of postsecondary education among a cross-section of society culminated in the Higher Education Act of 1965 (HEA). The HEA institutionalized federal support for higher education as a national interest and pledged that no student would be denied opportunities in higher education due to financial barriers. During the 1960s and 1970s, the expansion of opportunities in postsecondary education accelerated as a result of demands by historically excluded groups such as women and minorities for access to the socioeconomic mobility routes of higher education.

During the 1980s, federal higher education policy retracted from the historical concerns for equity in access, and the social benefits of a more educated citizenry were redefined as essentially private benefits. Individuals were encouraged to treat higher education as a necessary personal investment and to calculate the benefits of this investment in purely economic terms. From this perspective, higher education was primarily a private good because individuals with a college credential have a competitive advantage over other individuals.

Although financial aid reduces the amount of money college students must raise through work, family contributions, and other assets (such as a family home), not all forms of student aid are equally beneficial to individuals pursuing postsecondary education. During the past two decades, federal financial aid expanded considerably and currently represents a $60 billion annual invest-ment—yet the mechanism for the expansion in financial aid for college was student loans. Unlike grant financial aid, which reduces the price of college, loans actually *increase* the price of college due to the accrued interest students must pay. This shift in the federal commitment to financial aid from primarily grants to primarily loans echoed the new philosophy of higher education as a private good.

The overreliance on student loans to finance higher education, rather than expanding equal opportunity in higher education, rein-forces the U.S. stratification system. Individuals from disadvan-taged locations within the social hierarchies of race, class, and gender are more likely to borrow for college and are at increased risk for excessive educational debt burden after graduation. Furthermore, the overreliance on student loans conditions an instrumental consciousness that defines a college education as a "means-ends" rational investment. The debt acquired from the college experience results in pressure for students to find immedi-ate employment in order to repay their investments (i.e., student loans). Consequently, alternative choices for college graduates that privilege community interests over self-interest are deemed unreasonable.

This book is a call for a new social compact around higher education as a public good and for a more equitable distribution of the socioeconomic rewards of higher education. The social bene-fits of an increasingly educated citizenry should be justification enough for a renewed public commitment to equal opportunity in higher education. As the forces of global economic integration intensify, the importance of a college degree for entry into the pre-ferred labor market positions will only increase. The competition among various social groups for access to higher education repre-sents an important harbinger for the kind of society we wish to create in the twenty-first century. Will the United States continue to privilege individual self-interest in higher education policy with the consequence of increased polarization between the haves and the have-nots, largely shaped by race, ethnic, and class differ-ences? Or will it pursue the democratic vision of a more egalitari-an and meritocratic society and renew the collective commitment to opportunities in higher education? This book stakes out a trans-formative vision for higher education policy that can improve the well-being of all members of society, not simply the most privileged.

The Book Chapters at a Glance

Chapter 1 lays out the dual purposes of higher education from the philosophical standpoints of individual self-interest and collective common interest. The dual purposes of higher education have historical roots in the political writings of Thomas Jefferson, who believed that intellectual freedom and widespread educational opportunities were necessary conditions for political democracy. This chapter also lays out the basic perspective of the book: social reproduction theory. I explain that society is organized unequally and that individual actions are shaped by this unequal organization. Social inequality is measured as the relationships between race and ethnic groups, men and women, economic classes and their intersections. Public policy represents the way that social institutions can be used to encourage social reproduction or social transformation.

Chapter 2 explains the two trends in student financial aid that have come about over the past two decades: a transition from mostly grants to primarily loans, and the rising share of college costs that students and families pay. A brief review of federal financial aid policy is followed with data indicating that increased participation in higher education does not mean that gaps are closing in educational attainment among race, ethnic, gender, and income groups. The overreliance on student loans to finance higher education is contributing to education attainment gaps and undermining the balance between the individual and collective purposes of higher education.

In Chapter 3, the common misperception that poor and minority students attend college for "free" while middle-class and white students must borrow is shown to be false. Not only are African American, Hispanic, and lower-income students borrowing to pay for college, these students are more likely to adjust their college choices due to price and potential indebtedness and less likely to graduate from more prestigious colleges and universities. The data further illustrate that low-income students and African Americans are less likely to have earned a graduate or professional degree within four years of receiving a bachelor's degree. This lack of parity in educational outcomes is an indication of unequal opportunities in higher education.

In Chapter 4, the penalties associated with the successful pursuit of higher education credentials are explored. In particular, differences in the distribution of undergraduate and total educational debt burden across race, ethnic, class, and gender characteristics are examined. Moreover, the resulting educational debt burden once students enter the labor market is documented. The data show that students from lower-income families are more likely to have excessive debt burden than students from higher-income families, and black students are more likely to have excessive debt burden than white students. That is to say, low- and lower-middle-income students and black students who successfully attain a college degree are paying more for postsecondary education and thus receive a lower return on their investment in higher education. The increases in average educational debt levels over the past decade, and the increasing reliance on loans to provide financial assistance to students and families, very likely increased the total debt burden for more recent college graduates.

Chapter 5 revisits the work of Samuel Bowles and Herbert Gintis, whose book *Schooling in Capitalist America* (1976) documented the correspondence between students' class background and their ultimate destination in the labor market. The economic class distribution of undergraduate students from 1991 is compared to their class distribution in 1997 based on their income from employment. Although the range of class categories may reflect individual upward mobility, the group pattern after the attainment of an undergraduate or advanced degree is roughly equivalent. In colloquial terms, "if you entered college in the smallest boat, you're probably still in the smaller boat after you graduate." This chapter provides direct evidence that individuals may achieve upward mobility relative to their family's circumstances by receiving a bachelor's degree while at the same time the structural pattern of inequality among social groups during the life course continues to reflect race, ethnic, class, and gender characteristics.

Chapter 6 concludes that higher education represents both the promise of socioeconomic opportunity *and* the potential for inspiring agents of social change. The current overreliance on student loans to finance higher education creates an imbalance between these dual purposes of higher education. This imbalance diminishes the value of higher education as the social institution responsible for cultivating progressive ideas that can shape and transform society. In this chapter, I describe reforms that call for an integrated higher education policy across federal, state, and institutional levels. These innovative policies are informed by a philosophical vision for higher education that moves beyond the normative "means-end" framework fashionable among most political and economic elites. That is to say, federal and state policy regarding opportunities in higher education must be reinvigorated with the collective purpose of a more widely educated citizenry. Only in this way can the range of college and career choices for students, especially those with high financial need, be expanded and the dual purposes of higher education be rebalanced.

1 Higher Education and the Reproduction of Social Inequality

The reproduction of social inequality through higher education occurs against the backdrop of a two-decade trend in rising college prices that students and families are expected to pay, as well as the increased reliance on student loans to cover the corresponding rise in financial need. The consequence of a public policy that emphasizes the use of student loans to finance higher education is to alter the balance between the social and individual purposes of higher education. That is to say, requiring indebtedness to obtain a postsecondary education institutionalizes an antagonistic (rather than complementary) relationship between instrumental self-interest and communicative social interest.

Instrumental self-interest is the desire for individual mobility and the attainment of the American dream. *Communicative social interest* is the desire to contribute to the common good by improving the overall quality of life for all members of society. The reliance on student loans in federal financial aid policy privileges the individual value of higher education as a means to socioeconomic mobility, and it diminishes the collective value of higher education as a vehicle for social transformation. Thus, the pursuit of innovative and progressive ideas is diminished as a guiding principle of a college education; rather, the acquisition of educational skills valued in the marketplace becomes more important so that students can recoup their significant personal investment in higher education. This imbalance between the dual purposes of higher education contributes to the reproduction of social inequality.

The Dual Purposes of Higher Education

Higher education as a social institution provides both individual and societal benefits. For individuals with a college degree, real median earnings of full-time college educated workers increased by 16 percent between 1979 and 1999, while real median earnings of full-time workers with only a high school degree declined by 8 percent (Stiglitz et al. 2000). For society, higher education provides human capital (i.e., an educated citizen) that is associated with greater investments from global capital markets. These investments generate jobs that provide economic security because of their many favorable characteristics, such as high earning potential, health and retirement benefits, comfortable and safe working conditions, high employment status, and positive organizational environment (Galloway 1994; Gittleman and Howell 1995). An added social benefit of these jobs is a reduction in the demands for government-provided social services thanks to increased economic self-sufficiency.

Beyond the economic benefits that accrue to individuals as well as society, higher education also generates thoughtful social entrepreneurs and innovative thinkers whose ideas can transform society. Social entrepreneurs use higher education to develop more efficient and effective ways to provide basic human needs for more of the world's population. Innovative thinkers develop ideas that change the way individuals and groups view their roles in society, which can impact how society is organized. Society also benefits economically from education due to the resulting lower costs of social and economic infrastructure, a better social environment, a more effective political system, higher productivity, and the addition of wealth and employment to local communities (Carnoy 1993).

On the one hand, higher education offers certain skills that individuals can acquire and then exchange in the labor market for salaries, wages, and benefits. This private benefit of a college degree reflects higher education as a marketplace where individuals congregate as consumers to purchase the requisite credential needed to provide for their economic well-being. On the other hand, higher education is also the primary social institution where ideas can be freely exchanged and discussed on philosophical, cultural, and ethical grounds that are not generally welcome in the corridors of global capitalism due to its narrow focus on profit and capital accumulation. The communicative perspective informs these social and moral values of higher education.

Higher education, then, can be considered the central location where the instrumental values of individual mobility and economic benefits are balanced against the communicative values of producing informed citizens who develop social networks of mutual respect and understanding and whose actions can transform social reality. Experiencing this tension between the instrumental and communicative values of higher education shapes the actions of college graduates before, during, and after postsecondary education.

The Philosophical Foundations for the Social Value of Education

In the United States, the debate over the value of education and who should have access to what level of education can be traced to the revolutionary ideas that informed the Declaration of Independence and the formation of our democratic society. Thomas Jefferson believed that intellectual freedom and widespread opportunities in education were necessary conditions for political democracy. In his correspondence with John Adams of October 28, 1813, Jefferson advocated for basic education among broad segments of colonial society so that the natural aristocracy of men (i.e., one based on merit and ability) not be subjected to an artificial aristocracy founded solely on wealth and birth.[1] This vision for education was seen in the Bill for the More General Diffusion of Knowledge that Jefferson introduced in the legislature of the Commonwealth of Virginia in 1779. Although it was not passed into law, the legislation would have established a system of public schools to increase individual social mobility *and* to ensure the intellectual and moral capacity of all Virginians to protect the rights and freedoms fought for and won in the Revolutionary War (Ravitch 2001; Wagoner Jr. 1976).

John Dewey expanded on this notion of the collective value of education in his early-twentieth-century works on the relationship between schools and society. He recognized the tendency of people to view education from an individualistic perspective, but he also warned that this narrow understanding of schools would destroy democracy. "Individualism and socialism are at one" in the school, wrote Dewey. "Only by being true to the full growth of *all* the individuals who make it up, can society by any chance be true to itself" (Archambault 1964, p. 295, emphasis added).

Dewey's philosophy of education recognized that the conditions of life (e.g., the social and cultural environment) were constantly changing. The "ethical responsibility of the school on the social side must be interpreted in the broadest and freest spirit," wrote Dewey (Archambault 1964, p. 114). Education must teach individuals to adapt to the changes going on in society but also to have the power to shape and direct those changes (Archambault 1964). Thus, the institutions of education represented the mechanism through which society trained individuals to take responsibility for themselves and their families and also to act in ways to improve the collective well-being of all members of society. Like Jefferson, Dewey believed that this ethical foundation of education was the cornerstone of democracy and necessary for social and economic progress.

In the early twentieth century, both Dewey and Thorstein Veblen made similar arguments about the social value of higher education. In *Democracy and Education* (1916), Dewey asserted that the institutions of higher education were intended to transmit and conserve not the whole of a society's achievements but rather only those achievements that make for a better society. In a similar vein, Veblen emphasized in *The Higher Learning in America* (1918) that higher education should reflect a disinterested proclivity to gain knowledge in order to create a meaningful social system. In short, the idea that education serves both individual and collective purposes is not new; rather, it has a long political and intellectual heritage in American social thought. The critical point in understanding the dual purposes of education is that they are inseparable and that the social value must be primary for both individual and collective opportunities to flourish.

In the middle of the twentieth century, M. Baker (1966) interpreted Dewey and presumed three requirements of a democratic education. First, education must be a part of community life that all members of the community participate in fully and freely. Second, education must focus on the democratic perspective, which requires the educational environment to be experienced and viewed from the standpoint of humanity. Third, education must provide the community with a collective principle and purpose with the world, of which individual actions are intended to fulfill. Thus, education is intended to provide the means for individuals to pursue self-interest only insofar as those individual pursuits provide for the collective well-being and improvement of society as a whole. In other words, the purpose for educational institutions is to help individuals grasp their roles within a social framework while also developing each person's individuality (Ulrich 1970 [1940]).

More recently, Martha Nusbaum explained the purpose of education in the twenty-first century from the communicative standpoint by discussing higher education in the context of producing a world citizen. She wrote in *Cultivating Humanity* (1997) that

> [higher] education . . . must be a multicultural education, by which I mean one that acquaints students with some fundamentals about the histories and cultures of many different groups. These should include the major religious and cultural groups of each part of the world, and also ethnic and racial, social and sexual minorities within their own nation. Language learning, history, religious studies, and philosophy all play a role in pursuing these ideas. Awareness of cultural difference is essential in order to promote the respect for another that is the essential underpinning of dialogue. (p. 68)

In other words, the collective purpose of education must continue to be progressive and forward-looking, embracing the possibility of social transformation in order to improve the human condition as a whole.

This egalitarian and inclusive philosophical perspective of education is threatened when educational processes and structures restrict the ability of people to choose among different ways of life (Gutman 1998). If the balance between the dual purposes of education (i.e., the pursuit of both individual self-interest and communicative social interest) is an appropriate philosophical measure of a democratic education, then social science can investigate the structure of education from that standpoint. That is to ask, is the system of education "nonrepressive," meaning it neither sacrifices individual freedoms to communal virtue nor favors individual freedoms to the extent that the collective values essential to a just society are lost (Gutman 1998)?

*Outcome-Based Conceptions
of Equal Opportunities in Education*

The intended purpose of the Higher Education Act of 1965 and its subsequent amendments is to ensure that opportunities to pursue postsecondary education are not denied to any capable person who wishes to pursue education beyond high school. It follows logically that the empirical measure of equal opportunities to pursue higher education is one of parity. That is to ask, do different groups of people pursue higher education in similar proportions? Furthermore, among different groups who do pursue higher education, is equality present among relevant outcome measures? Kenneth Howe states this principle as follows: "Parity between groups of individuals is required on all educational outcomes that affect an individual's chances to enjoy other social goods" (1998, p. 212). Put simply, equal opportunities in education are present when the structural conditions of education allow for parity on important educational outcomes among various social groups.

It is my contention that the overreliance on student loans to finance higher education, in fact, undermines equal opportunities in education. In order to provide empirical evidence to support this argument, I presuppose two fundamental concepts: first, that the social system in the United States is unequal; and second, that the social system shapes the actions of individuals and groups within the higher education system. These two premises represent a philosophical and theoretical worldview that places a high value on egalitarianism as a social good. The lack of parity among groups of individuals on several educational outcomes (college enrollments, distribution of college attendance, educational attainment, and educational debt burden) indicates the existence of unequal opportunities in education. This unfairness regarding opportunities in higher education contributes to the reproduction of social inequality.

Theoretical Framework

In any given historical epoch, the actions people take either reproduce the existing social order or create alternatives to and thus transform the social order.[2] These actions are always constrained by existing structural realities. This understanding of the historical

The Higher Education Act of 1965

In 1965, the U.S. Congress passed the Higher Education Act (HEA), which was intended to expand opportunities for postsecondary education. According to section 400 of the HEA, the purpose of federal financial aid programs is "to assist in making available the benefits of postsecondary education to eligible students." An eligible student is qualified for admission to an institution of higher education and maintains satisfactory progress consistent with the graduation requirements of that institution. Every five years, HEA is reauthorized, and amendments are often added that change the scope of funding for student financial aid, for state-federal partnerships, and for institutional support. Title IV of HEA authorizes student financial aid programs, including Pell Grants, Supplemental Education Opportunity Grants, College Work Study, Perkins Loans, and guaranteed student loans (i.e., Ford Direct Loan Program and Federal Family Educational Loan Program). Title IV also provides funding for support services targeted to disadvantaged students through the federal TRIO programs and through state-federal partnership grants (i.e., Gaining Early Awareness and Readiness for Undergraduate Programs, or GEAR-UP). Titles III and V of HEA provide support to historically black colleges and universities, Hispanic-serving institutions, and tribal colleges. The next reauthorization will occur during the 108th Congress in 2003–2004.

process recognizes that society is organized unequally and that more powerful groups use institutional structures in ways that enable them to maintain their privileged positions. This is not to say that social change is impossible or that existing structural realities are immutable; on the contrary, history is rife with examples of human actors effectively challenging unequal social relationships. At the same time, the decisions of human actors are shaped within hierarchical institutional contexts.

Individuals navigate through higher education informed by

two primary factors. The first factor is the experience of individuals as interpreted through the inequalities of race, ethnicity, class, and gender within the social system. The second factor is federal and state higher education policies, which represent the structural conditions of higher education. In other words, public policy articulates the framework through which individuals make choices about higher education. The outcomes of these choices can be documented by the race, class, and gender characteristics of individuals.

Figure 1.1 illustrates conceptually how structural patterns of inequality can coexist with individual upward social mobility. Consider three points along a time continuum. At any given point (1, 2, 3), a parity gap exists between the 2 groups. Between points 1 and 2, and points 2 and 3, both groups improve their outcome positions from the previous point; however, the parity gap between the groups grows larger. Hence, mobility within a given group can improve while the gap between the groups grows larger. The between-group measure of parity represents the structural pattern of inequality. The within-group measure of a given outcome represents the individual pattern of social mobility.

Defining the Social System

The social system of the United States is unequal; race, ethnicity, class, and gender represent the predominant social relationships of

Figure 1.1   Theoretical Mapping of Structural Patterns of Inequality and Individual Patterns of Social Mobility

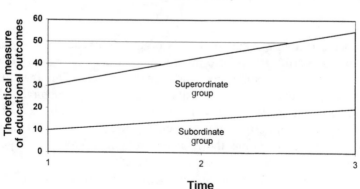

this inequality. This theoretical perspective recognizes both the differences of race, class, and gender, *and* the systemic links among race, class, and gender categories (see, e.g., P. Collins 1998, 1991; West 1997; Chow 1996; West and Fenstermaker 1996; Andersen and Collins 1995; Young and Dickerson 1994; D. King 1988). Moreover, the analytic categories of race, class, and gender represent *both* privileges and disadvantages dependent upon the sociocultural situation and on the particular set of race, class, and gender intersections. Thus, inequality within the U.S. social system can be measured and documented by investigating the distribution of resources (such as higher education credentials, occupations, and salaries) attributable to particular race, class, and gender intersections. Each of these analytical categories expresses an unequal relationship between social groups, which favors the dominant and disfavors the subordinate.

In his classic work *Caste, Class, and Race* (1948), Oliver Cromwell Cox defined an ethnic or racial group as a people living competitively in relationships of "superordination" or "subordination" with respect to some other people or peoples. In this view, race is not skin color but rather an indicator of a relationship among groups of people whose interactions are experienced as privilege and disadvantage. In the U.S. social stratification system, for example, the analytical category of race can measure the unequal relationship between blacks and whites. For blacks, race is a category of disadvantage that is manifest through institutional discrimination and personal prejudices in everyday life. For whites, by contrast, race is a category of advantage: they have historically benefited from their forbearers' access to land, decent-paying jobs, and wealth at a time when most African Americans were excluded from such resources (Oliver and Shapiro 1995). In addition, regardless of economic inequality, whites often exhibit attitudinal superiority to ethnic and racial minority groups who, as a whole, are worse off (Feagin and Vera 1995).

Similarly, the analytic category of gender measures the relationship between men and women that is generally experienced as privilege for men and disadvantage for women. For example, one scholar (Jacobs 1996) found that women remain disadvantaged in their access to elite schools even though the per capita share of women's enrollment in the United States exceeds that of most other countries. In terms of occupational opportunities after college, others (Fuller and Schoenberger 1991) found that for business graduates income differences remain stratified by gender in first full-time jobs. Furthermore, it has been found (see Wilson and Boldizar 1990) that women were still concentrated in college curriculum fields with the lowest mathematics achievement and the lowest income potential. Gender inequalities persist even among the most affluent students: despite the disproportionate attendance of elite boarding school (EBS) graduates in selective colleges, more EBS men than women attend selective colleges (Persell, Catsambis, and Cookson Jr. 1992).

Class also measures a series of unequal relationships; however, it is more difficult to link the analytic concept of class with an empirical indicator. In the traditional sense, the concept of class reflects the relationship of people to the means of capital accumulation. In this view, one is either an owner who does not need to work or a worker who must sell his or her labor in order to survive. An empirical definition of class must accept the centrality of class position in determining access to the resources of society (see Wright 1997, 1985); thus class is generally measured in terms of income, which indicates the relative opportunity of nonowners to purchase the goods and services necessary for livelihood. Not only are financial resources a prerequisite for opportunities such as opening a small business, the lack of wealth relegates individuals, families, and social groups to wage-earning activity. Moreover, without some assets there is no safety net for the economically marginal family to protect itself against month-to-month fluctuations in income or in necessary expenditures (Spilerman, Lewin-Epstein, and Semyonov 1993). It is the inequalities among these groups of workers (hourly, salaried, and professional) that define the class relationship empirically.

This framework of the social system as one of unequal relationships indicated through the intersections of race, class, and gender avoids the pitfalls of essentialism, reductionism, and one-dimensionality that often hinder empirical research (McCarthy and Crichlow 1993). Essentialism defines race, class, or gender as homogeneous categories that indicate a universal experience rather than as the heterogeneous categories they actually are. Indeed, experiences of gender, race, or class are not universal but reflect both privilege and disadvantage depending on the sociocultural situation.

Reductionism defines race, class, or gender categories as byproducts of some other category: most commonly, race and gender inequality are described as functions of class inequality. Yet women and racial and ethnic minorities do not receive the same benefits of higher-income status in all circumstances, as do their white male counterparts. A few common examples include the well-dressed African American male who is unable to hail a taxi, or the black driver who is pulled over by the police because he "doesn't belong" in a particular neighborhood.

One-dimensionality follows from essentialism and reductionism by defining race, class, or gender only by privilege or disadvantage. Thus, a privilege for higher-income groups is generalized to all individuals within the category without regard to race or gender. Yet it is more precise to recognize that the privileged relationship of men to women cannot be separated from the disadvantaged relationship of blacks to whites or of poor people to middle-income people. For instance, the experiences of a middle-income African American male are different from a middle-income white male because the former is black and the latter is white.

The pitfalls of essentialism, reductionism, and one-dimensionality stem from the same flawed conceptualizations of the analytical categories of race, class, and gender as static and disconnected attributes of individuals. In actuality, these categories represent relationships among groups that are unequal; that vary depending upon the particular institutional context; and that can and do change over time. Thus, the social system is defined as a system of hierarchies (namely, race, class, and gender) that operate together to create and reinforce opportunities for some individuals while reproducing disadvantages for others.

Social Structure Limits Social Change

The structure of the unequal social system further shapes the agency of individuals and groups within society. *Structure* is defined here as the relationships of social institutions—such as family, education, government, and the labor market—to one another. *Agency* refers to the behavioral choices of individuals and is often described as "free will," or the freedom to make decisions based on the information available. Structure and agency are not independent of one another. Rather, individual behaviors occur within particular institutional environments.

Put another way, society is organized unequally, and individual actions are shaped by this unequal organization. Social inequality is measured as the relationships between race and ethnic groups, between men and women, between economic classes, and their intersections. Public policy is a tool by which social institutions encourage the reproduction of social inequality or allow for possibilities of social transformation. Because higher education can improve opportunities for individuals and benefit society, it represents the sociocultural situation for this analysis. In this context, student loans represent the specific manifestation of public policy that reinforce systematic patterns of social inequality and thus limit the possibilities of social change.

Financial Aid and Postsecondary Opportunities

Federal financial aid policy plays the central role in regulating the conditions through which students choose to attend and complete a college education. In the first place, federal grant and loan aid represents two-thirds of available financial aid for students. This claim is further supported by more than twenty years of research on the effects of student financial aid on college enrollments. This research has consistently documented that students need help in paying for college and that financial aid positively affects college access (Heller 1999; R. Thomas 1998; St. John 1991, 1990; Murdock 1987; Blakemore and Low 1985, 1983; Manski and Wise 1983; Jackson 1978). Student financial aid also helps students stay in school and complete their objectives (Perna 1998; St. John 1989; Terkla 1985). In particular, need-based grant programs positively affect access, achievement, and graduation for low-income students (St. John et al. 2002; McCreight and LeMay 1982; Bergen and Zielke 1979).

Despite the generally positive effects of financial aid on college access and completion, the continued combination of tuition increases and the reliance on student loans may limit choices for those student populations who continue to be underrepresented in colleges and universities (Kane 1999; Heller 1996; St. John 1991; Davis and Johns 1989). According to a 1991 survey by the American Council on Education, 70 percent of respondents indicated that student loans were essential for college enrollment, and 45 percent claimed that loans enabled enrollment at their college of choice (Boyd and Wennerdahl 1993). Yet earlier research

(Schwartz 1985) found that low-income students are often unwilling to incur debt because of the fear of default. A more recent study (Cofer and Somers 2000) found that higher student debt levels are associated with increased withdrawals from college. Furthermore, a 2002 survey of college borrowers found that a larger proportion of black (44 percent) and Hispanic (51 percent) borrowers felt loans limited their college choices compared to white (35 percent) borrowers (Baum and O'Malley 2003).

Research has documented that the redistribution of financial aid from primarily grants to primarily loans in the 1980s resulted in a shift of low-income students to lower-priced four-year and two-year colleges, while middle-income students also shifted to less expensive institutions (St. John and Eliot 1994). Another study (McPherson and Schapiro 1998) examined the patterns of college enrollments across institutional type between 1980 and 1994 and found that enrollments at public two-year colleges had increased for lower-income students but had decreased for all other (i.e., higher-) income groups. Put another way, freshman enrollments at public and private four-year colleges declined for students with family incomes below the median from 52 percent and 42 percent to, respectively, 41 percent and 35 percent between 1981 and 1993 (Davis 1997). In fact, freshman enrollments for these students declined at all colleges by seven percentage points during this decade. Moreover, the gap in college participation by family income has not closed over the past thirty years. In 1970, about 80 percent of eighteen- to twenty-four-year-olds in the top income quartile were enrolled in college compared to less than 50 percent of eighteen- to twenty-four-year-olds in the lowest income quartile (College Board 2002a). By 2000, this gap had not closed, although a higher proportion of all eighteen- to twenty-four-year-olds were enrolled in college.

The basic relationship between college prices and college enrollment is that as the price of college goes up the probability of enrollment tends to go down.[3] Specifically, increases in tuition and decreases in financial aid lead to declines in college enrollment and completion; lower-income students are more sensitive to such changes. Black students and community college students are also more sensitive to changes in tuition and financial aid than are white students and students in four-year public colleges and universities, respectively.

In addition, for those students who borrow to finance their

college educations, there is concern about the ability to pay back student loans. In one survey of college borrowers (The Institute for Higher Education Policy and The Education Resources Institute 1995), more than 50 percent of respondents indicated that additional debt or a major expense would pose a serious financial risk to their household. Another survey of student borrowers (Baum and Saunders 1998) found that for students who finished their degree program, 40 percent of students with debt delayed purchasing a home, 31 percent delayed purchasing a car, and 22 percent delayed having children. A more recent survey of student borrowers found that 41 percent of low-income borrowers felt that loans limited their college choices, and 39 percent of low-income borrowers responded that loan repayments caused more hardship than anticipated (Baum and O'Malley 2003). This research suggests that encouraging students to borrow to attend college is not without consequence for equal opportunities in higher education.

Reproducing Inequality Through Higher Education

Despite significant and growing investments in student financial aid, the opportunity to pursue higher education is not equally available to all capable students. According to the Advisory Committee for Student Financial Assistance (2002), which is chartered by the U.S. Congress to monitor postsecondary opportunities and federal student financial aid programs, in any given year more than 170,000 college-qualified low-income students are unable to attend any postsecondary institution due to financial barriers. That is to say, many students who are prepared for college cannot attend because they lack the financial resources.

The opportunity to obtain the necessary skills and ability to be admitted to a four-year college or university is also denied to many Americans because of inequities among public primary and secondary schools. And there is a reason why disadvantaged groups do not have the same chances to prepare for postsecondary education: public education is funded by personal and business property taxes. This funding mechanism requires communities with lower property values to pay higher taxes than communities with higher property values in order to generate comparable revenues for schools. According to a report from the National Center for Education Statistics (National Center for Education Statistics 1998b), revenues per student in schools serving households with a median income of less than $22,000 were less than $5,400 after federal support was included. In contrast, revenues per student in schools serving households with a median income greater than $38,000 was more than $5,900 without any federal support; once federal support was included, schools serving more affluent households had $6,650 in revenues per student (National Center for Education Statistics 1998b). These figures illustrate a 19 percent revenue gap between schools serving the wealthiest and the poorest households.

This inequity in public financing of primary and secondary education has implications for students attending these schools. For example, only 21 percent of high school graduates from families with income less than $25,000 were "highly" or "very highly" qualified for college based upon their secondary school curriculum (National Center for Education Statistics 2000b). In contrast, 56 percent of high school graduates from families with income greater than $75,000 were "highly" or "very highly" qualified for college (National Center for Education Statistics 2000b). Put more bleakly, almost half of all high school graduates from families with incomes less than $25,000 were not qualified for college compared to only 14 percent of high school graduates from families with incomes greater than $75,000 (National Center for Education Statistics 2000b).

A recent national report from the Indiana Education Policy Center further illustrates the lack of equal opportunities in higher education that faces even college-qualified lower-income students (St. John 2002). Despite widespread expectations to finish college among all students, 61 percent of college-qualified low-income students take an entrance exam and apply for college; 19 percent do not take an entrance exam and do not apply; and 17 percent take an entrance exam but do not apply. In contrast, almost 91 percent of high-income students take an entrance exam and apply for college; less than 3 percent do not take an entrance exam and do not apply (St. John 2002). Thus, even low-income students who are college-qualified are not taking the necessary steps to apply and enroll in college proportionate with high-income college-qualified students.

Despite the unequal access to higher education, more and

more students are enrolling in college. In fact, more students from all race and ethnic backgrounds are enrolling in college and earning a postsecondary degree. Yet the gaps in college enrollments and graduation among different race, ethnic, and income groups are growing larger. Thus, the paradox of college access is that trends in enrollment and attainment are positive for all students, but the gaps between students from privileged and disadvantaged backgrounds are also increasing. Furthermore, students from disadvantaged race, ethnic, and economic class backgrounds are more likely to face greater debt burden after they graduate from college.

Educational Opportunities and the Impact of Student Loans

Table 1.1 provides a snapshot of the pathway to educational attainment and socioeconomic opportunities for students from different race and ethnic backgrounds. At virtually all points along this pathway to opportunities, a larger proportion of white students are present relative to the national average, and a smaller proportion of students from African American and Hispanic backgrounds are present. This illustrates how systematic patterns of inequality associated with race and ethnic characteristics remain despite individual examples of educational achievement and upward social mobility. This lack of parity among different groups of individuals is an indication of unequal opportunities in higher education. One of the primary reasons for this pattern of inequality is the overreliance on student loans to finance postsecondary education.

Federal student loans are entitlements available to all qualified students. Federal grant aid, by contrast, must be appropriated through the legislative process. This regulatory imbalance between different types of financial aid encourages borrowing as the primary mechanism for students to pay for college. The consequence of this imbalance between grant aid and loan aid is that it penalizes African American, Hispanic, and lower-income students by limiting their decisions during the transitions from high school to college to career.

For students who are academically prepared for college, the

Table 1.1   Race and Ethnic Inequalities Along the Education and Economic Opportunity Pathway

	H.S. Completion Rates, 18 to 24 Years Old (percentage), 1995	College Enrollment, 18 to 24 Years Old (as percentage of H.S.graduates), 1999–2000	College Graduate with B.A. Degree, 25 Years Old and Older (percentage), 2000
White	89.8	45.3	17.0
National	85.3	43.7	15.5
African American	84.5	39.2	9.5
Hispanic	62.8	31.6	6.7

	College Graduates with Advanced Degree, 25 Years Old and Older (percentage), 2000	Median Income, Full-Time Workers, 25 to 34 Years Old, 2001 ($)			
		H.S. Graduate	B.A. Degree	M.A. Degree	Doctorate Degree
White	9.8	27,463	41,107	47,268	49,031
National	8.9	26,164	40,777	48,126	46,980
African American	4.8	23,310	36,018	39,723	40,584
Hispanic	3.8	23,666	36,230	44,010	51,996

Sources: U.S. Bureau of the Census (2002), U.S. Bureau of the Census (2003), National Center for Education Statistics (2002a).

choice of where to attend is strongly influenced by the price of the different institutions. The sticker price for college varies significantly between public and private institutions because of significant state investment in public two-year and four-year colleges. According to the College Board (2002a), the average price of attending public four-year colleges was $8,991 in 2001–2002 compared to $23,751 at private four-year colleges. Between 1992–1993 and 1999–2000, the net price (after all grant aid) students were expected pay increased to $11,344 at public research and doctoral universities and increased to $21,713 at private research and doctoral universities (National Center for Education Statistics 2002c). Net price also increased slightly to $9,287 at public comprehensive and undergraduate institutions.

Only after loan aid was awarded did net price to students decline between 1992–1993 and 1999–2000. Thus, students are relying more on loans to pay for college. Alongside this increased reliance on educational loans, the net price students must pay after all financial aid remains significant. For example, unmet need for low-income students is more than $4,500 to attend a public four-year comprehensive and undergraduate institution; more than $5,600 to attend a public four-year research or doctoral university; and almost $11,000 to attend a private four-year research or doctoral university (National Center for Education Statistics 2002c).

The increasing prices that students are paying for college after grant aid, and the subsequent reliance on loans, have influenced the decisions that students make about where to attend college. A report from the ECMC Group Foundation (2003) found that lower-income students have a greater aversion to financing higher education with borrowed money. This report concluded that the discomfort with educational loans among low-income students could be restricting their educational options beyond high school. Similarly, MATHTECH Inc. (1998) analyzed parental attitudes toward debt and concluded that debt-averse parents, especially those from lower-income backgrounds, have children who are less likely to attend postsecondary education.

Academic researchers have also explored the impact of borrowing on college choices. It has been found that lower-income students and race and ethnic minorities are increasingly attending less-expensive four-year colleges and two-year community colleges, in part to avoid borrowing (St. John and Eliot 1994). Thus, many students are adjusting their college choices as a consequence of federal financial aid policy, and these adjustments are more likely to be made by African American, Hispanic, and lower-income students. Ironically, even if loan-averse students begin their postsecondary education at community colleges, they are just as likely to incur large amounts of debt if they obtain a bachelor's degree. Unfortunately, less than 40 percent of students who enroll in a community college with the intention of obtaining a bachelor's degree make the transition to a four-year college (Choy 2002).

If students obtain a bachelor's degree, the educational debt amassed affects the decision whether to pursue graduate education or enter the labor market. Students possessing large debt are less likely to apply for graduate or professional school. Moreover, students who borrow as undergraduates are less likely to obtain a graduate or professional degree. The level of indebtedness also impacts the initial return on the investment in higher education because loans must be paid back once a student is no longer enrolled in a degree-seeking educational program. Although these negative consequences of educational debt affect all borrowers, African American, Hispanic, and lower-income students are disproportionately represented among students whose decisions are limited as a result of borrowing for college.

Despite these unequal conditions, students from all race, ethnic, and class backgrounds are attending college in larger numbers and obtaining postsecondary credentials. However, disparities in the amount borrowed to obtain a bachelor's degree or a graduate degree, as well as ongoing disparities in labor market salaries received by different groups of individuals, combine to create problems of educational debt burden. Educational debt burden refers to the percentage of gross monthly income required to service the principle and interest of educational debt. The rule of thumb is that 8 percent represents the maximum reasonable debt burden students should have to face. Unfortunately, a significant minority of students have educational debt burden that exceeds this threshold; once again, lower-income students and African Americans are more likely to face this negative consequence of borrowing for college.

The chapters that follow address the pathway to educational attainment and socioeconomic opportunities. At each transition point along this pathway, students from different race, ethnic, gender, and class backgrounds must make important decisions that will impact their chances to obtain social goods indicative of upward individual mobility. Additionally, students will make choices about the way society should be organized in order to expand or limit opportunities for future generations. Unfortunately, overreliance on student loans to finance higher education opportunities creates new inequalities for groups of individuals already in disadvantaged positions within the social system. The reality of student debt not only undermines the promise of equal opportunities in higher education; it also creates structural conditions that encourage the reproduction of social inequality.

Notes

1. The letter is available online at presspubs.uchicago.edu/ founders/documents/v1ch15s61.html.

2. The theoretical premise for this book was developed from my dissertation. D. V. Price (1999), "Systems of Inequality: Student Indebtedness and Early Labor Market Incorporation" (Washington, DC: American University).

3. The *price* of college refers to the tuition, fees, books, supplies, room and board, etc., that students and their families pay to attend a college or university. The *cost* of college refers to the actual expenditures for educational purposes by colleges and universities. In virtually all cases, the price of college is less than the cost of college because of subsidies provided by federal, state, and local governments, and private donations to colleges and universities.

2 The Promise of Higher Education and the Reality of Student Debt

A s discussed in Chapter 1, the promise of higher education as a social institution where progressive ideas can shape and transform society is constrained by the structural realities of financing one's education. The federal legislation that sets the tone for financial aid policy in the United States is the Higher Education Act of 1965. The HEA authorizes student financial aid programs such as the Pell Grant, the Federal Family Education Loan Program, and the Ford Direct Student Loan Program; it is reauthorized every five years. Current practice in federal policy treats student loans as entitlements intended to be the primary mechanism by which students pay for college. Thus, to compete for preferred positions within the global labor market by obtaining a college degree, many students must first borrow money to pay for college. The result is personal indebtedness that amplifies students' need for preferential labor market incorporation.

Although higher education provides the opportunity for individuals to overcome disadvantage and improve socioeconomic status relative to their parents, the pattern of inequality among college graduates continues to reflect race, class, and gender characteristics. The reason for this reproduction of social inequality is the overreliance on borrowing among college-educated men and women, combined with ongoing labor market inequalities between men and women and among race and ethnic groups. The manifestation of this limitation is twofold. First, equal opportunities to enter higher education are denied to disadvantaged social groups, particularly African Americans, Hispanics, and individuals from lower-income backgrounds. Second, significant financial penalties accrue to college graduates who pursue public service occupations or other low-paying, but socially valuable, careers.

The Imbalance Between
Individual and Collective Interests

In contemporary U.S. society, the balance between the individual and communicative benefits of higher education is under duress. The underlying structural cause of the current imbalance is the interplay between three factors:

1. The increased share of college costs that students and families are expected to pay;
2. The overreliance on loans to finance these additional costs; and
3. The ongoing race, ethnic, gender, and class inequalities in the labor market.

During the past two decades, the proportion of education and general expenditures at institutions of higher education paid for by students and families has increased from 27 percent to 36 percent (see Figure 2.1). During this same period, the state and local share declined from 44 percent to 34 percent. The federal share has remained stable around 16 percent since 1985–1986. Thus, tuition and fees now represent the largest single source of revenues used for education and general expenditures by colleges and universities. This shift in how the costs of higher education are shared made college less affordable for more families. Between 1990 and 2001, average tuition at public four-year colleges rose faster than median income in 41 states (National Center for Public Policy and Higher Education 2002). Put another way, between 1991–1992 and 1999–2000, the average price of attendance increased by 21 percent in real dollars at public four-year colleges and by 24 percent at private four-year colleges (College Board 2002a). Median household income increased by only 13 percent during this same period, which means that financial need increased alongside rising college prices.

Figure 2.1   Percentage Share of Education and General Expenditures of Degree-Granting Institutions Covered by Federal, State, and Local Appropriations and by Tuition and Fees, 1980–1981 to 1995–1996

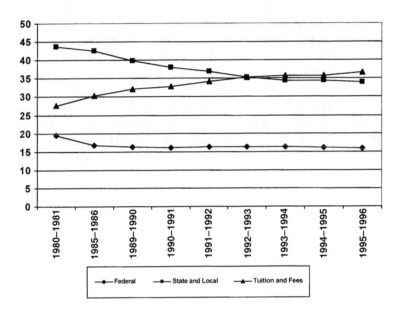

Source: National Center for Education Statistics (2002a), tables 330 and 341 (author calculations).

This increase in the price of college for students and their families has been paid primarily by loans. In 2001–2002, student loans accounted for $41 billion of the $54 billion in federal financial aid awarded to college students—an increase of 195 percent since 1991–1992 (College Board 2002b). The distribution of federal student financial aid has changed dramatically over the past quarter-century. In 1976–1977, student loans represented only 18 percent of total federal student aid (Institute for Higher Education Policy 1998) compared to 78 percent of total federal student aid in 2001–2002. Between 1991–1992 and 2001–2002, the Federal Family Education Loan Program and Ford Direct Loan Program more than doubled from about $14 billion annually to more than $36 billion in constant dollars (College Board 2002b). In contrast, the largest federal grant aid programs (Pell Grants and Supplemental Educational Opportunity Grants [or SEOG]) grew by only 31 percent during this same period (College Board 2002b).

Although the individual returns on a college education are much higher compared to the economic returns on a high school diploma, significant differences in average income remain between college-educated men and women and among race and ethnic groups. According to data from the U.S. Census Current Population Survey (March 2002), the 2001 average earnings for full-time women workers between twenty-five and thirty-four years of age with a bachelor's degree was $42,230 compared to almost $55,000 for men. A similar gap existed between whites, blacks, and Hispanics: full-time black and Hispanic workers between twenty-five and thirty-four years of age with a bachelor's degree had average earnings of $42,093 and $42,804, respectively, in 2001 compared to $49,486 for white workers. See Figure 2.2.

A Brief History of Financial Aid Policy

The trends in federal financial aid during the past two decades were not unavoidable or solely the result of market forces. On the

Figure 2.2   Average Earnings for College-Educated Full-Time Workers, 25 to 34 Years Old, 2001

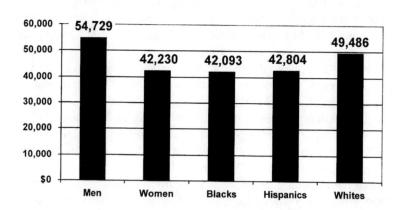

Source: U.S. Bureau of the Census (2002).

contrary, federal and state public policy regarding higher education has been deliberate—although not widely debated. During the 1980s military buildup under Republican president Ronald Reagan, the expansion of the guaranteed student loan program provided increased financial aid for students for a much lower per-student cost to the government compared to the per-student cost of federal grants. Loans are less expensive as public policy because the government pays only interest and default costs. The consequence of this shift, however, is the transformation of federal student aid from a policy of creating equity in access (a social goal) to the current policy of encouraging students to invest in their own future by saving and/or borrowing for higher education (an individual goal).

This shift away from traditional concerns for equity in access occurred during the 1980s and can be considered as Reagan's legacy to federal higher education policy. Federal student aid was transformed from a policy of creating access to disadvantaged social groups to one of broadening choice and providing convenience for the middle class (J. King 1996). The new orientation of higher education policy became one of excellence, selectivity, productivity, competition, and devolution (Clarke and Astuto 1990; St. John and Eliot 1994). In other words, the focus of federal policy is now toward universal access to some form of postsecondary education rather than for equal participation among different groups of students (Hansen and Stampen 1994). In short, federal policy lost its philosophical coherence as a result of the convolution of individual educational attainment with social benefits (Hearn 1993).

State student aid policy followed the federal shift away from social equity and toward individual opportunity through the development of merit-based financial aid programs in lieu of larger increases in (or creating new) need-based financial aid programs. According to the 2001–2002 survey by the National Association of State Student Grant and Aid Programs (National Association of State Student Grant and Aid Programs 2003), state non–need-based financial programs are growing significantly faster than state need-based programs and now make up 26 percent of all state aid dollars. This change in state financial aid policy reflects competing demands for state budget dollars as well as reduced revenues due to tax cuts. Between 1990 and 1995, mean state funding of higher education declined about 0.5 percent annually, whereas Medicaid rose 10 percent annually, prison spending rose 8.5 percent annually, primary and secondary education spending rose 3.7 percent annually, and state welfare programs rose 1.6 percent annually (reported in Mumper 2001). In the decade ending in 2000, real per-capita spending in states increased 32 percent nationally; health and corrections spending grew significantly faster while higher education spending grew significantly slower (D. Boyd 2002).

The dual purposes of higher education—one based on the communicative value of pursuing ideas to improve social systems, the other focused on the instrumental value of obtaining skills to improve an individual's competitive position within the social system—are mirrored in the development of federal higher education policy during the post–World War II era. In 1947, the President's Commission on Higher Education, appointed by President Harry Truman, issued its final report articulating the promise of higher education to mean a more educated civilian population; it also called for the removal of financial barriers to higher education. President Dwight Eisenhower's 1960 Goals for Americans report called for the expansion of the community college system, expanded development of doctoral programs, state planning for an improved public higher education system, and further investments in student financial aid through grants and loans. The first of three programs to help first-generation and low-income students pursue higher education, Upward Bound, was created by the Economic Opportunity Act of 1964. Two additional programs, Talent Search and Student Support Services, later complemented Upward Bound in 1965 and 1968, respectively. As mandated by Congress, two-thirds of the students served by these TRIO programs must come from families with incomes less than $24,000 in which neither parent graduated from college.

The Higher Education Act of 1965 institutionalized federal support for higher education and specified the objectives of federal support: knowledge-building through expanded research capacity, curriculum and training support in languages, health care and libraries, and direct support to students through financial aid programs. In 1968, a report by the Carnegie Commission directed by Clark Kerr reinforced the value of providing greater equality of educational opportunity as an important public good. The development of these programs, which emphasized the importance of college access for an increasing number of students, emerged from the belief that expanding access to higher education was a worthwhile social investment.

The implementation of the GI Bill, federal grants, student loan services, and increased direct subsidies by state governments represented an academic "revolution" in higher education, according to Roger Geiger (1999), professor of higher education at Pennsylvania State University. This revolution was facilitated by the convergence of several social, political, and economic factors. First, businesses were demanding a more highly trained workforce and expected universities to be the primary source for cutting-edge research and the training of workers, especially in the emerging computer technology fields. Second, politicians wanted education to be available for all "capable" Americans in order to win the space race against the Soviet Union, which had earlier successfully launched the Sputnik satellite. Third, groups historically excluded from higher education, including women and racial and ethnic minorities, working through the broader civil rights and women's liberation movements, demanded that the mobility routes of education be opened and expanded.

The watershed in federal financial aid policy occurred in 1972 with the introduction of market-based formulas for individualized financial aid packages. The HEA amendments that year formalized the federal government's commitment to provide need-based financial aid to help students and their families pay for college. In addition to the Pell Grant (renamed in 1980), this legislation established the government-sponsored enterprise known as the Student Loan Marketing Association (Sallie Mae) in order to create incentives for private banks to provide low-interest loans to students to attend college. Sallie Mae provided a secondary market for student loans by purchasing the student loan portfolios of private lenders as long as those lenders made new loans to students totaling 125 percent of the initial portfolio.

The creation of Sallie Mae indicated that access to higher education would be accomplished by a new partnership between businesses and government. This partnership represented the political and economic consequences of the changing public discourse on higher education. No longer was the emphasis on the value of large-scale social investments that benefited all of society;

instead, the discourse surrounding federal higher education policy (namely, student financial aid) was framed as the means for individual students to pursue and achieve self-interested goals.

This private-public partnership is very profitable for the lenders who participate. According to the U.S. General Accounting Office, until 1992 lenders received 100 percent insurance for the amount of loans in default (since reduced to 98 percent), including principal and interest, which effectively socialized the risk. Sallie Mae's historical status as a government-sponsored enterprise implicitly guaranteed "the full faith and credit of the United States" as the financial underwriter for its total debt.[1] Thus, private lenders are guaranteed their principal loan amounts against default by the U.S. Treasury, receive subsidized interest payments while the student is in school, and before repayment begins can transfer the risk of loan default to the tax-paying public. In this sense, the use of student loan markets to provide financial aid for students is a type of corporate welfare. Lenders provide loan capital for students for a limited but guaranteed rate of return, yet the investment risks remain with the federal government.

This arrangement is also more cost-effective for the federal government. Because the private capital market provides the principal loans for college students, federal government outlays are needed only to cover subsidized interest and default costs. For instance, this policy can leverage $10 billion in student loans for approximately $1.5 billion in subsidized interest charges, loan default costs, and administrative expenses (15 percent of $10 billion).[2] By contrast, the Pell Grant program is exclusively funded by federal government appropriations and is comparatively more costly. Thus, the absolute value of $11.9 billion in funding for Pell Grants, Supplemental Educational Opportunity Grants, and College Work Study (CWS) in 2001–2002 was significantly greater than the approximately $3.9 billion necessary to support the $26 billion in student loans administered through the Federal Family Education Loan Program.

Throughout the 1980s and 1990s, amendments to the HEA and other legislation led public policy farther down this instrumental path by reforming need-based analysis for student aid, expanding loan maximums, and creating new loan programs. In 1981, Parent Loans for Undergraduate Students (PLUS) were introduced; they provided a low-interest option for parents who borrowed to help pay for their children's college education. In 1986, borrowers were granted the right to consolidate their loans for longer terms at lower interest rates, which actually increased the cumulative interest borrowers paid on their educational loans. In 1992, the unsubsidized Stafford Loan was given entitlement status; borrowers are responsible for paying the in-school interest that accrues on these loans. By 1993, lenders were required to offer "income-sensitive" loan payments, which are based upon a percentage of a borrower's annual income. In 1995, the Direct Student Loan Program was implemented (this program awarded $11.4 billion in student loans in 2001–2002; College Board 2002b). Between 1975 and 2000, the loan portion of federal financial aid dollars almost tripled while Pell Grant appropriations fell 50 percent in real dollars. Since the inception of the student loan program, the federal government has guaranteed more than $400 billion in student loans.

Higher Education: Attainment, Enrollment, and Cost

In 2003, state governments contributed almost $64 billion to institutions of higher education, according to the Center for Higher Education at Illinois State University. Tom Mortenson (1998) documents, however, that state appropriations from tax revenues for higher education per $1,000 of state personal income have declined by 30 percent since 1979. According to the American Association of State Colleges and Universities, direct state appropriations per student remains at 1978 levels in constant dollars (McKeown-Moak 1999). During the same period, tuition and fees paid by students and families covered 40 percent of the increase in educational and general expenditures by institutions of higher education.

College Enrollments

Despite the increasing share of costs that students and their families are expected to pay, the number of college-educated men and women is greater today than at any time in U.S. history. According to the National Center for Education Statistics, between 1972 and 2000 the percentage of high school graduates immediately enrolling in college the October after completing high school increased from 49.2 percent to 63.3 percent. In raw numbers, total undergraduate enrollment in degree-granting post-secondary institutions increased from 7.4 million students in 1970 to almost 12.7 million students in 1999 (National Center for Education Statistics 2002a). Increased enrollments have occurred for men as well as women. Men's enrollment increased to 5.5 million in 1999 from 4.25 million in 1970, and women's enrollment increased from 3.1 million to more than 7 million. This growth in enrollment occurred across all institutional types: public four-year enrollments increased by 39 percent, private four-year enrollments increased by 66 percent, and public and private two-year enrollments increased by 138 percent. See Figure 2.3.

These patterns of increased college enrollments vary considerably by income and race, and significant gaps remain in the percentage of high school graduates who enroll in college immediately after completing high school. Despite gains in college enrollments for all race and ethnic groups, the gap between white and black students increased from 5 percent in 1980 to 8 percent in 1999. An even larger increase in the gap occurred between

Figure 2.3　Percentage of High School Graduates Who Were Enrolled in College the October After Completing High School, 1980–1999

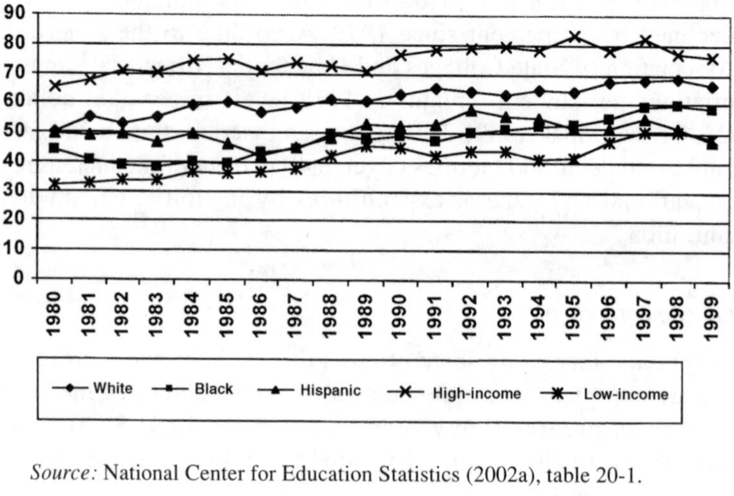

Source: National Center for Education Statistics (2002a), table 20-1.

whites and Hispanics during this period. Between 1980 and 1999, the gap between low-income and high-income students barely changed, hovering between 28 percent and 33 percent. In 2000, the college participation gap between low-income and high-income students between eighteen and twenty-four years old was almost 30 percent—the same level recorded in 1970 (College Board 2002a).

According to the U.S. Census Bureau, 39 percent of all white eighteen- to twenty-four-year-olds were enrolled in a degree-granting institution in 1999. The comparable rates for African Americans and Hispanics were 30 percent and 19 percent, respectively. These differences in enrollment rates between income and racial/ethnic groups reveal a looming demographic problem for higher education in the twenty-first century. U.S. Census data show that the population of African Americans grew 16 percent to 33.9 million and that the Hispanic population grew 58 percent to 35.4 million between 1990 and 2000. These fast-growing groups have the lowest rates of educational attainment and the highest dropout rates.

Educational Attainment

Although the anticipation of higher earnings may encourage students to enroll in an institution of higher education, college graduation rates suggest that this incentive does not ensure degree attainment. According to the American College Testing Service (ACT), the five-year graduation rate at public and private four-year colleges was 51.2 percent in 2000, 4 percentage points lower than in 1987. More strikingly, the five-year graduation rate at public four-year colleges declined from 48.5 percent in 1987 to 41.9 percent in 2000. Put simply, college enrollments are improving but college graduation rates are declining. Researchers at UCLA's Higher Education Research Institute (Astin et al. 1996) sampled 60,000-college freshmen in 1985 and found that the six-year graduation rate for white students was 47 percent, but the rates for African Americans and Mexican Americans were 34 percent and 40 percent, respectively. Thus, less than half of the students who enroll in college actually receive a bachelor's degree; this completion rate is worse for race and ethnic minorities.

Figure 2.4 shows the cohort graduation rate at colleges and

Figure 2.4   NCAA Division 1 Cohort Graduation Rates, 2000

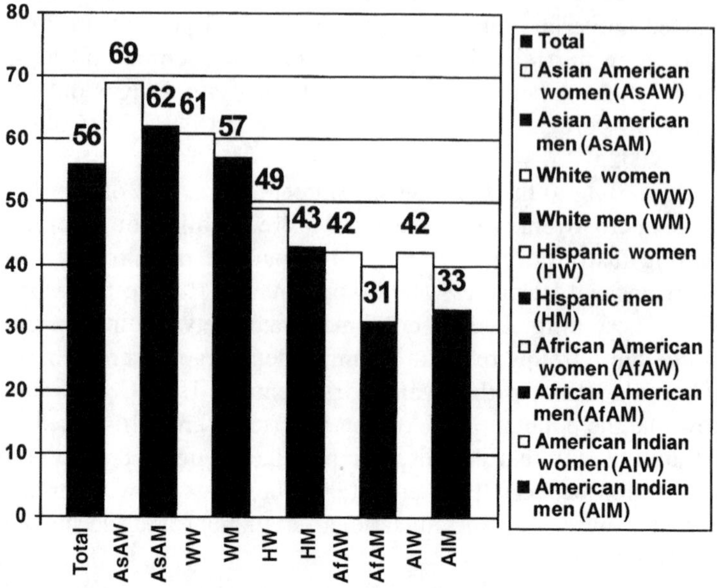

Source: American Council on Education (2002a).

universities in 2000, as reported to the National Collegiate Athletic Association by Division I postsecondary institutions. The overall graduation rate for all students was 56 percent, but significant differences remain according to race, ethnic, and gender characteristics. For example, 61 percent of white women graduated within five years compared to 57 percent of white men. In contrast, only 49 percent of Hispanic women and 42 percent of African American women graduated within five years. Even fewer African American men (31 percent) and Hispanic men (42 percent) earned a bachelor's degree within five years in 2000.

These considerable differences in college enrollment and completion rates result in educational attainment inequalities between race and ethnic groups. Data on persons of Hispanic origin are not available before 1974: in that year, 4 percent of Hispanic women and 7 percent of Hispanic men had completed at least four years of college. About 6 percent of African American men and 5 percent of African American women had completed at least four years of college in 1974. The comparable rate for white women and men was 18 percent and 11 percent, respectively. By 2000, the attainment gap between white, black, and Hispanic men had increased: almost 31 percent of white men had completed at least four years of college compared to 16 percent of African American men and 11 percent of Hispanic men. Similarly, the attainment gap between white, black, and Hispanic women also increased during the past thirty years. In 2000, 26 percent of white women had completed at least four years of college compared to 17 percent of African American women and 11 percent of Hispanic women. See Figures 2.5 and 2.6.

Despite such differences, the overall trend in educational attainment confirms the value people place on higher education. In 1970, 11 percent of adults age twenty-five years and older had completed at least four years of college. By 2000, more than 25

Figure 2.5   Race and Ethnic Gaps (%) in Male Population 25 Years Old and Older with at Least a Bachelor's Degree, 1970–2000 (selected years)

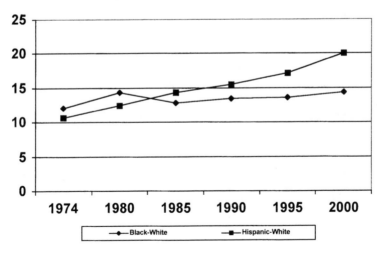

Source: U.S. Bureau of the Census (2003) (author calculations).

Figure 2.6   Race and Ethnic Gaps (%) in Female Population 25 Years Old and Older with at Least a Bachelor's Degree, 1970–2000 (selected years)

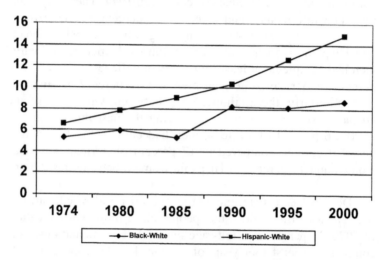

Source: U.S. Bureau of the Census (2003) (author calculations).

percent of adults had completed at least four years of college. This measure shows that the percentage of college-educated adults more than doubled during the past thirty years. These national educational attainment rates vary by gender. In 1970, 14.1 percent of men twenty-five years and older, but only 8 percent of women, had completed at least four years of college. This gender gap is smaller but still present in 2000: 28 percent of men twenty-five years and older had completed at least four years of college compared to 24 percent of women. The percentage of college-educated men doubled during the past thirty years, and the percentage of college-educated women tripled.

Wage Premiums

An important benefit of higher education is that a college credential can change the kinds of choices an individual faces. For example, the labor market offers college graduates a significant wage premium. In 1999, U.S. Census data showed that the median earnings gap between a full-time college-educated male worker and a high school–educated male worker increased to 70 percent from 29 percent in 1979. For full-time female workers, the college premium increased to 83 percent from 42 percent. In 2001, the median earnings for college-educated full-time male workers between twenty-five and thirty-four years old were slightly more than $46,000 compared to $29,247 for high school–educated workers. Similarly, median earnings for a college-educated full-time female worker were almost $37,000 in 2001 compared to $22,452 for a high school–educated worker (U.S. Bureau of Census 2002). The slower growth in the college wage premium for women may in part reflect the significant growth in college-educated women's labor force participation, and the higher wage premium for women is likely a function of the significantly lower wages of non–college-educated women.

At the same time, the choices for college-educated individuals are not equally expansive for all college graduates because the labor market remains differentiated along ethnic and gender dimensions. Although average earnings for college-educated men twenty-five and thirty-four years old who worked full-time in 2001 were $54,729, women's earnings were only $42,230. In other words, college-educated women earn 77 cents for every dollar earned by college-educated men. Similarly, the average earnings for college-educated blacks and Hispanics twenty-five to thirty-four years old who worked full-time in 2001 were $42,093 and $42,804, respectively, or 16–18 percent less than the $49,486 average earnings for whites (see Figure 2.2).

This inequality in the labor market is especially troubling because the pathway to expanded opportunities through higher education requires borrowing for most of its participants. According to *Unequal Opportunity: Disparities in College Access Among the 50 States* (Kipp, Price, and Wohlford 2002), low-income students in particular must borrow to gain access to higher education. In twenty-two states, less than half of public institutions are accessible without borrowing for low-income traditional-age students (eighteen to twenty-four years old); these affordable institutions are primarily two-year community colleges. For adult students at least twenty-five years old, there is virtually no loan-free access to higher education in the fifty states and the District of Columbia.

Rising College Costs

The numerical growth in educational attainment for all demographic groups during the past two decades has occurred alongside significant growth in the price charged to college students by institutions. The National Center for Education Statistics reports that between 1989 and 1999 the cumulative price of college paid for by students increased from $18,200 to $31,300 at four-year public colleges, and from $44,500 to $78,100 at private four-year colleges. According to the Lumina Foundation for Education (2002), the majority of the additional charges at four-year public colleges were paid for by student loans during this period: 95 percent of the increased charges to students between 1991 and 1995, and 62 percent of the additional charges between 1995 and 1999. Consequently, the average debt for four-year public college graduates almost tripled in the past decade from $5,848 to $14,200. Average debt more than doubled for private college graduates, from $7,551 to $15,400. See Figure 2.7.

Figure 2.7   Average Undergraduate Tuition and Fees and Room and Board Rates ($) Paid by Full-Time Equivalent Students, 1989–1999

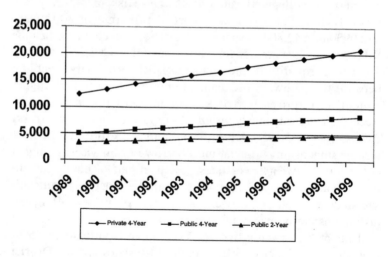

Source: National Center for Education Statistics (2002a), table 313.

Public Policy Shapes Individual Choices

Given the increased reliance on student loans to finance higher education, the pre- and post-undergraduate decisionmaking process is necessarily shaped by the debt graduates will accrue if they attend college. The reality of student debt limits the possibilities of social transformation and progress by imposing socioeconomic consequences on the choices students make about whether to attend college, where to attend college, what to study while in college, whether to continue with graduate education, and what kinds of career opportunities to pursue. That is to say, because of the impact that borrowing has for one's economic status, the decisions that students make after college are more limited for borrowers than for nonborrowers. What makes this situation especially troubling is that patterns of student borrowing vary by race, gender, and class characteristics among students. African Americans, Hispanics, and students from lower-income families are more likely to be influenced by the need to borrow for college and are more likely to face excessive educational debt burden early in their careers. Thus, the reality of higher education opportunities for disadvantaged students is the necessary accumulation of educational debt.

Notes

1. In 2008, Sallie Mae will become completely independent of the federal government.

2. Some estimates suggest that the cost of loan programs is 50 percent of total loan value. These estimates raise serious questions about the federal commitment to grant aid, because they imply that money spent on administering loan programs is greater than the dollars invested in federal grant programs. See E. P. St. John (2003), *Refinancing the College Dream: Access, Equal Opportunity, and Justice for Taxpayers* (Baltimore: Johns Hopkins University Press).

3 Educational Attainment: The Effects of Public Policy and Student Borrowing

C hapter 2 provided aggregate data that suggested how trends in state appropriations to higher education, as well as the shift in federal financial aid to primarily loans, influenced the patterns of educational attainment over the past decade. Although state governments increased their subsidies to higher education during this period, such increases have not sufficiently provided for the growth in college enrollments. According to a recent report from the National Center for Education Statistics, decreasing revenue from state appropriations was the most important factor associated with tuition increases at public four-year institutions between 1988–1989 and 1997–1998; this study also found that tuition levels at private, not-for-profit four-year colleges were related to the price of attending a public institution in the same state (National Center for Education Statistics 2001d).

The consequence of the declining share of state appropriations directed toward higher education is higher tuitions: in 2001–2002, the average total price of attendance was $23,751 at private four-year colleges and universities and $8,991 at public four-year institutions (College Board 2002a). After adjusting for inflation, these prices were 38 percent higher than in 1988–1989 at private colleges and 33 percent higher at public colleges. According to *Losing Ground,* a 2002 report from the National Center for Public Policy and Higher Education, the percentage of income required to pay for one year of college almost doubled for low-income families, from 13 percent to 25 percent, between 1987 and 2001.

Accompanying these rising tuitions is the significant growth in federal student financial aid. The federal government provides more than two-thirds of all available financial aid for higher education. According to the College Board report *Trends in Student Aid* (2002b), total federal aid exceeded $54 billion in 2000–2001, of which more than 77 percent consisted of student loans. Indeed, the buying power of the Pell Grant declined from covering 98 percent of public tuition in 1987 to covering just 57 percent of public tuition at four-year colleges in 2001, which increases the need for students to use loans to pay for college (National Center for Public Policy and Higher Education 2002). In 2001–2002 more than 5.7 million students participated in federal student loan programs, which represents a 48 percent increase in the number of borrowers since 1993 (College Board 2002b). Thus, higher tuitions are increasingly paid with loans, and this overreliance on loans impacts the college choices of students as well as their future education and career decisionmaking.

These two trends—the rising price of college that students and families are expected to pay, and the resulting debt levels associated with attending college—are influencing educational attainment patterns. That is, students are adjusting their college choices to attend less expensive, and generally less prestigious, colleges and universities because of high prices and the need to borrow. These choices impact the opportunity to pursue graduate education and also influence the returns college graduates receive from the labor market. For example, elite schools disproportionately channel graduates into lucrative careers and confer direct benefits on graduates independent of personal characteristics (Kingston and Smart 1990). Thus, between-college effects strongly influence labor market outcomes because more prestigious educational credentials enhance the probability of upward ascent within senior management ranks of U.S. corporations (Useem and Karabel 1990).

Factors That Influence Educational Attainment

Several studies have documented that economic class background represents the most significant influence on educational attainment for white, African American, and several Asian American ethnic groups (Goyette and Xie 1999; Duncan 1994; Bowles and

Gintis 1976). This upper-class advantage in obtaining higher educational credentials has created a "credential society." That is, the process of credential inflation, which increases the educational requirements for the best jobs, favors the most privileged students who are most able to obtain such credentials (R. Collins 1979). Upper-class students are more successful in getting professional credentials than their less advantaged counterparts despite equal precollege aspirations, self-image, and college grades. The college credential thus becomes the gatekeeper to corporate employment because it is used as a screening device to gauge success in a competitive environment, and it is perceived to represent a certain set of social and personality skills (Useem 1989). Given the importance of economic class in obtaining an elite college credential, education becomes the mechanism for the transfer of advantage from generation to generation (Ganzeboom, Treiman, and Ulte 1991). Put another way, upper-class origin not only increases the likelihood of attending an elite institution, it also confers a significant advantage to the career prospects of senior managers with the same educational credentials (Hearn 1990). Consequently, the "credential society" reinforces the comparative advantage of class-privileged individuals.

Although billions in federal financial aid are provided to help students pay for college, such aid is not closing the educational attainment gap between lower- and higher-income students or among African Americans, Hispanics, and whites. One reason that federal financial aid is not effectively closing educational attainment gaps is the overreliance on educational loans; these loans further increase the price students and families pay for college because the interest on student loans adds to the total price of a college education. Students who borrow money to cover college expenses pay a 33 percent premium on the portion of college paid for by student loans (assuming a standard ten-year payback at 7 percent annual interest). According to the Government Accounting Office (2003), average cumulative undergraduate educational debt exceeded $18,000 in 2000, which corresponds to a $6,000 premium borrowers pay for a college education.

In 2000, the National Center for Education Statistics released a longitudinal database of a nationally representative sample of college graduates. This database, *Baccalaureate and Beyond 1993/1997* provides information on family background,[1] total educational debt, the types of financial aid packages graduates received, the level of educational attainment, and the prices colleges charged students.[2] In addition, several national studies using the *National Educational Longitudinal Survey* and the *High School and Beyond Survey* have documented the college-going patterns of secondary school students. These data can be used to examine basic questions of social equity in higher education, including: (1) the relationship between college prices, borrowing, and attendance patterns; (2) the relationship between borrowing and family background variables; (3) the relationship between average educational debt, college attendance patterns, and family background variables; and (4) the relationship between borrowing and graduate educational attainment.

Attendance Patterns:
College Prices and the Reliance on Student Loans

Students from lower-income families face a college affordability crisis. These students are increasingly underrepresented in four-year colleges and universities, and their college participation rates are declining (Davis 1997). During the past decade, the proportion of freshmen from families with income in the lowest quartile that enrolled in private four-year colleges and universities declined slightly and the proportion that enrolled in private universities and public four-year colleges remained stable. Yet low-income freshmen remain largely underrepresented at private four-year colleges and universities and overrepresented at public two- and four-year colleges (Davis and Wohlford 2001).

On average, 38 percent of students who enrolled at public baccalaureate institutions of higher education in 1999 received a Pell Grant, as did 34 percent of students who enrolled at public comprehensive college and universities (Lumina Foundation 2003a). In contrast, less than 32 percent of students who enrolled at private baccalaureate institutions of higher education in 1999, and only 28 percent of students who enrolled at private comprehensive colleges and universities, received a Pell Grant. At public and private doctoral universities, only 25 to 27 percent of students enrolled in 1999 received a Pell Grant. Thus, public baccalaureate and comprehensive colleges and universities disproportionately enroll low-income students.

Data from the National Center for Education Statistics confirm that students from low-income families are less likely to enroll in four-year colleges and universities. In addition, fewer African Americans and Hispanics attend four-year colleges than do whites. Moreover, significant gaps in college attendance rates remain between African Americans and whites; between 1976 and 1992, this gap actually increased (National Center for Education Statistics 2001a). Among 1992 high school graduates, only 33 percent of students from low-income families enrolled in a four-year college by 1994, compared to 47 percent of middle-income students and 77 percent of high-income students (National Center for Education Statistics 1998a). Similarly, 31 percent of Hispanic high school graduates enrolled in a four-year college by 1994, compared to 42 percent of African Americans and 47 percent of whites (National Center for Education Statistics 1998a).

One reason for the difference in where students attend college is that lower-income students and African American students are more sensitive to the prices colleges charge (Heller 1997; Leslie and Brinkman 1987). A recent study on the impact of state policies on the college enrollment patterns of high school graduates found that states with low public college and university tuitions have higher enrollments in public four-year institutions (Perna and Titus 2002). A $1,000 difference in state public two-year college tuitions is associated with a 7.2 percentage point decline in college enrollments for low-income students; the same difference in state public four-year tuitions is associated with a 4.4 percentage point decline in college enrollments for low-income students (Kane 1999). According to one study (McPherson and Schapiro 1998), the consensus among econometric research is that a $150 increase in net costs reduces college enrollment rates for low-income students by 1.8 percent.

The significant increases in family resources needed to pay for college during the past decade had a disproportionate impact on students from lower-income, African American, and Hispanic families (Heller 2001b). In fact, average net tuition after grants for African Americans and Hispanics increased by 208 percent and 414 percent, respectively, between 1989 and 1995; the increases in net tuition for students from the lowest two quintiles of family income also increased more compared to net tuition for higher income families during this period (Heller 2001b). Given current trends in college prices, a family with an income of $45,000 would need to save 10 percent of its income for eighteen years in order to afford to send one child to a private college or university (Kane 1999). Therefore, reducing the trend toward higher tuitions may be necessary to expand the college enrollment rates among students from disadvantaged positions within the social system.

A second reason for the difference in where students attend college is that borrowing is more likely at more expensive colleges and universities. The data from *Baccalaureate and Beyond* confirm the relationship between borrowing, educational debt, and the prices students are expected to pay for college. That is, tuition and fees, the total price for a full-time student, and student budgets are all positively associated with borrowing. Although the correlation statistics are not strong, it is common sense that borrowing is more likely at colleges and universities with higher prices.

Put another way, students who borrowed for college attended more expensive institutions, on average, compared to students who did not borrow for college. Figure 3.1 illustrates that the tuition and fees paid by student borrowers were more than 10 percent higher than the tuition and fees paid by nonborrowers.

Figure 3.1   Average Annual Price of Undergraduate Education Between Borrowers and Nonborrowers, 1992–1993

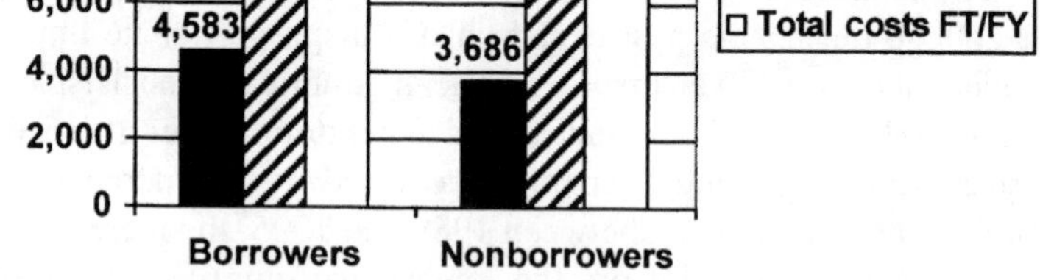

Source: National Center for Education Statistics (2000a).
Note: P < .001 t-test for Equality of Means

The higher prices paid by borrowers is also present when comparing student budgets and total price. For example, the total price paid by borrowers for one year of college was $12,450 compared to $11,774 for nonborrowers. The relationship between college prices and college attendance patterns suggests that borrowing at higher levels is more likely if students want to attend higher-priced and often more prestigious colleges and universities.

The decision to attend less expensive colleges generally results in students choosing public comprehensive colleges rather than research and doctoral institutions. Figures 3.2 and 3.3 illustrate that students from low-income, African American, and Hispanic backgrounds as well as women disproportionately graduate from comprehensive colleges and universities. These patterns are generally true for both public and private four-year colleges. For example, 23 percent of private four-year college graduates are from research and doctoral institutions; however, only 16 percent

Figure 3.2 **Proportion of College Graduates at Private Research, Doctoral, Comprehensive, and Liberal Arts Institutions by Race, Ethnicity, Gender, and Economic Class Background, 1992–1993**

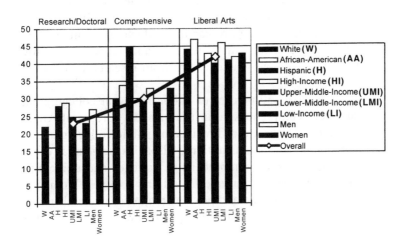

Source: National Center for Education Statistics (2000a).
Note: See Appendix for tables.

Figure 3.3   Proportion of College Graduates at Public Research, Doctoral, Comprehensive, and Liberal Arts Institutions by Race, Ethnicity, Gender, and Economic Class Background, 1992–1993

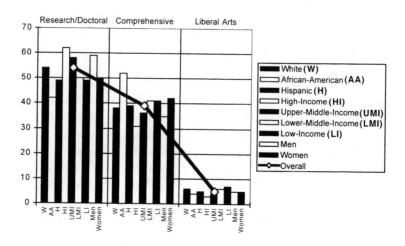

Source: National Center for Education Statistics (2000a).
Note: See Appendix for tables.

of African American private college graduates are from research and doctoral institutions. Similarly, 53 percent of public four-year college graduates are from research and doctoral institutions, but only 42 percent of African Americans and 49 percent of low-income public college graduates are from research and doctoral institutions.

Thus, whereas 39 percent of public four-year college graduates are from comprehensive institutions, 52 percent of African American and 41 percent of low-income public college graduates are from comprehensive institutions. Hispanics are generally overrepresented at private comprehensive colleges and universities and underrepresented at private liberal arts colleges. Women are overrepresented at public and private comprehensive colleges and underrepresented at public and private research and doctoral institutions.

In contrast, 62 percent of high-income students who graduated from private four-year colleges, and 29 percent of high-income students who graduated from public four-year colleges, attended research and doctoral institutions. Yet only 25 percent of high-income public four-year college graduates and 31 percent of high-income private four-year college graduates attended comprehensive colleges. Thus, one manifestation of the overreliance on loans to finance higher education is that lower-income students and African American students, by choosing less expensive colleges and universities, are less likely to graduate from research and doctoral institutions and more likely to graduate from comprehensive colleges. By graduating from these institutions, students can reduce their cumulative educational debt, but they also may limit their opportunities to pursue a graduate education; these decisions can impact early career salaries and long-term socioeconomic mobility.

Average Undergraduate Educational Debt

Although low-income, African American, and Hispanic students disproportionately attend less expensive colleges, in part to reduce their perceived need for loans, they still accumulate significant educational debt. In fact, for many students educational loans help finance higher education no matter what college they attend. Regardless of the total annual price of college, more than half of all students who graduated from college in 1992–1993 had educational debt one year later. A recent study of 1993 college graduates (Heller 2001a) found that African Americans, Hispanics, and students from families with incomes less than $50,000 had lower cumulative undergraduate debt compared to white students and students from families with incomes greater than $50,000. In fact, total undergraduate debt ranged from $8,274 for Hispanics to $9,751 for African Americans and $10,475 for white students. Low-income and lower-middle-income students had average undergraduate debt of $10,261 and $10,057, respectively, compared to an average undergraduate debt of $11,241 for high-income college graduates (see Table 3.1).

However, average debt for all students was not significantly different between graduates of the lowest-priced and highest-priced colleges and universities. With the exception of African American students, graduates of lower-priced colleges and universities borrow slightly larger amounts compared to students who

Table 3.1   **Average Undergraduate Educational Debt Among 1992–1993 College Graduates**

	Overall ($)	Highest-Priced Institutions ($)	Lowest-Priced Institutions ($)
Race and ethnicity			
White	10,475	10,558	10,632
African American	9,751	11,027	9,143
Hispanic***	8,274	5,838**	7,966
Economic class			
High-income	11,241	10,865	11,048
Upper-middle-income	10,540	10,534	10,566
Lower-middle-income*	10,057	9,927	10,241
Low-income*	10,261	10,291	10,407
All students	10,339	10,301	10,443

Source: National Center for Education Statistics (2000a).
Notes: *** Statistically different from whites (P < .001)
** Statistically different between high- and low-priced institution (P < .05)
* Statistically different from high-income (P < .05)

attend higher-priced colleges. Table 3.1 shows that African American graduates from low-priced colleges graduate with more than $9,100 in educational debt, on average, compared to more than $11,000 in total undergraduate debt for African American graduates of high-priced colleges and universities. This difference is not statistically significant but may be of considerable practical significance for African Americans choosing where to attend college. In contrast, Hispanic graduates of low-priced colleges and universities borrow significantly more compared to Hispanic graduates of high-priced institutions. This fact could explain why Hispanics are overrepresented at research and doctoral institutions, which tend to have higher prices (i.e., Hispanics may receive significant grant aid at higher-priced research and doctoral institutions, which reduces the need for student loans). In general, the differences in average total undergraduate debt between low-priced and high-priced colleges and universities are not statistically significant, varying a few hundred dollars, but are slightly higher at lower-priced institutions.

Determining Financial Need: A Primer on Need Analysis

The most commonly used formula for determining eligibility for federal financial aid programs (see Kane 1999) is called the Federal Methodology, which calculates an expected family contribution (EFC) considered reasonable according to a family's income, other assets (e.g., investments), family size, and dependency status. The application of this formula to demonstrate financial need is called "need analysis." (Need analysis has different eligibility thresholds for dependent and independent students. In 1992, the definition of "dependency" was clarified: only those students older than twenty-four, veterans, married students, graduate students, orphans, or those who have children of their own are considered independent.) Students and their families must fill out the Free Application for Federal Student Aid to determine their eligibility for federal financial aid programs. Until 1992, the Federal Methodology formula included the largest single noncash asset most families own: their home. (An alternative formula, the Independent Methodology, still includes students' or families' home when determining financial aid eligibility. The Independent Methodology generates a higher EFC than the Federal Methodology and is used by many private colleges and universities to award institutional financial aid.) In calculating the EFC, available income is defined using the adjusted gross income from a family's federal tax form in the most recently reported year. Families are given an income allowance based on their family size and number of students in college. Families are also given an asset protection allowance based on the parents' ages and number of adults in the household. Any family income above the protected amount and 12 percent of assets above the allowance are considered available resources for financing a college education. The EFC is based on a progressive tax rate of unprotected income and assets. These rates range from 22 percent for the first $11,000 to 47 percent of any amounts exceeding $22,100. Since assets and income are a function of one's economic class position, financial aid rewards are generally correlated with student and family income.

These data suggest that students from different race, ethnic, and economic class backgrounds respond differently to the need for student loans to finance higher education. In simple terms, more affluent students and white students may embrace loans to expand college choices, whereas lower-income, African American, and Hispanic students may limit their college choices due to fears about accumulating large amounts of loan debt. Ironically, despite choosing less expensive and generally less prestigious colleges and universities, students from disadvantageous locations within the social system still accumulate significant undergraduate debt levels. Thus, on the one hand, lower-income and African American students must borrow to attend less-expensive colleges and universities. On the other hand, borrowing provides upper-income students and white students an opportunity to attend colleges they might otherwise be unable to afford. These choices about where to attend college can impact the opportunity to pursue a graduate education.

Graduate Educational Attainment, College Choices, and Student Debt

Given the increasing number of students with bachelor's degrees, the college where one receives educational credentials and the level of one's educational attainment are increasingly important factors in the competition for preferred labor market positions. The need for high-paying jobs is further exacerbated by the large educational debt students accumulate in paying for college. The most recent data from the Government Accounting Office indicate total undergraduate debt exceeding $18,000 in 2000, which is almost double the level of debt for 1992–1993 college graduates in the *Baccalaureate and Beyond 1993/1997* sample.

According to the U.S. Census, workers with graduate and first-professional degrees earn considerably more than workers with only bachelor's degrees. Figure 3.4 illustrates that full-time workers twenty-five to thirty-four years old with a master's or doctorate degree had median incomes of $48,126 and $46,980, respectively, in 2001, compared to a median income of $40,777 for workers with only a bachelor's degree. The wage premium for a graduate degree is considerable, ranging between 15 and 20 per-

Figure 3.4 Median Annual Earnings ($) for Full-Time Workers 25 to 34 Years Old by Educational Attainment, 2001

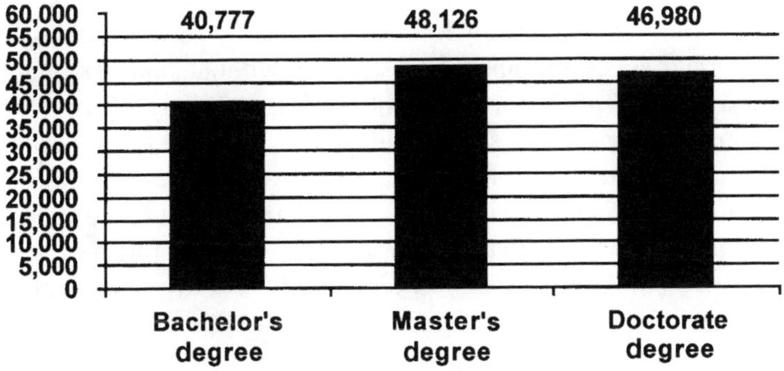

Source: U.S. Bureau of the Census (2002).

cent. Thus, college graduates can increase their earnings by obtaining a graduate degree. Unfortunately, the overreliance on loans to pay for higher education influences low-income and African American students to attend less expensive comprehensive colleges and universities. Graduates from such colleges are less likely to obtain an advanced degree. The need to borrow for a college education also influences the pattern of graduate educational attainment among college graduates four years after they received a bachelor's degree.

Patterns of Graduate Educational Attainment Among Dependent Students

Research on the impact of student debt on post-baccalaureate decisions of college graduates has been mixed due to limitations in the available data (see Millet 2003 for a detailed review). Independent students are typically older than twenty-four and pursue a bachelor's degree in order to improve the socioeconomic circumstances for their family. I focus on dependent students in this section because they are following the historical pattern of educational attainment from high school to college and on to a graduate institution. Two recent studies that used the *Baccalaureate and Beyond 1993/1997* longitudinal database of 1992–1993 college graduates found that student borrowing and undergraduate debt are related to application and enrollment in graduate school. Millet (2003) found that students with debts ranging from $10,000 to $15,000 were 40 percent less likely to apply to a graduate or professional school compared to students without undergraduate debt; students with debts of $5,000 to $10,000 were 60 percent less likely to apply. One study (Heller 2001a) found a significant difference in the proportion of students who were enrolled in graduate school and borrowed as undergraduates (40 percent), versus the proportion of students who were working full-time and borrowed as undergraduates (50 percent). This study also found a slight negative effect of cumulative undergraduate debt on graduate school enrollment in 1994.[3]

A small minority (16 percent) of dependent undergraduates who received a bachelor's degree in 1992–1993 obtained a graduate or professional degree by 1997. These data indicate that undergraduate borrowing was not statistically associated with obtaining an advanced degree within four years of receiving a bachelor's degree. In fact, about half the students with graduate or professional degrees had educational debt as undergraduates. Even so, dependent college graduates from research and doctoral institutions were overrepresented among graduate or professional degree recipients, whereas graduates of comprehensive colleges and universities were underrepresented among graduate or professional degree recipients in 1997. Low-income, African American, and Hispanic students are more likely to graduate from comprehensive institutions. Moreover, one in five dependent students from high-income families earned a graduate or professional degree by 1997 compared to only one in seven college graduates from low-income families.

The *Baccalaureate and Beyond 1993/1997* longitudinal survey is an ideal data source to test the relative impact of undergraduate borrowing, the type of undergraduate institution attended (i.e., research/doctoral or comprehensive), and family background characteristics on the probability of receiving a graduate or professional degree four years after earning a bachelor's degree. Since the outcome of interest is a binary variable (the student did or did not have a graduate or professional degree), logistic regression is the appropriate technique to generate probability estimates.[4]

Figure 3.5 illustrates the probabilities that dependent students

Figure 3.5   Likelihood of Obtaining a Master's or First Professional Degree Within Four Years of Receiving a Bachelor's Degree, 1992–1993 College Graduates

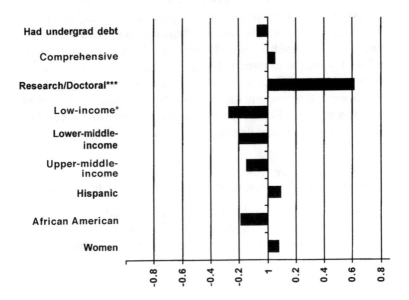

Source: National Center for Education Statistics (2000a).
Notes: *** P < .001, * P < .05
See Appendix for tables.

from different race, ethnic, and economic class backgrounds obtained an advanced degree by 1997.[5] College graduates from low-income backgrounds are 1.3 times *less* likely than high-income students to have received a graduate or professional degree within four years of receiving a bachelor's degree. In contrast, graduates from research and doctoral colleges and universities, who are disproportionately from high-income families, are 1.6 times *more* likely to have received a graduate or professional degree by 1997.

Because low-income students and African American students attend less expensive comprehensive colleges and universities in order to reduce undergraduate debt, but still accumulate significant levels of educational debt, it is reasonable to further examine the distribution of students with graduate or professional degrees who borrowed as undergraduates. Figure 3.6 illustrates that 68 percent of dependent students from low-income families who obtained a graduate or professional degree, and 59 percent of students from lower-middle-income families, borrowed as undergraduates compared to only 23 percent of students from high-income families who obtained an advanced degree. Similarly, 79 percent of African American students with an advanced degree in 1997 borrowed as undergraduates compared to only 48 percent of white students and 54 percent of Hispanic students who obtained a graduate or professional degree.

Educational Debt Levels Among Graduate and Professional Students: Race, Class, and Gender Inequality

Borrowing for college did not directly inhibit students from low-income, African American, or Hispanic families from obtaining a graduate or professional degree. In fact, given the limited availability of grant financial aid, student loans were necessary for

Figure 3.6   Percentage of Students with a Graduate or Professional Degree in 1997 with Undergraduate Educational Debt, 1992–1993 College Graduates

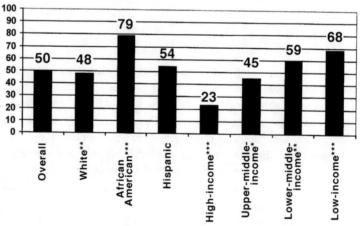

Source: National Center for Education Statistics (2000a).
Notes: *** P < .001, ** P < .01, * P < .05

those students to pursue graduate education. Thus, all but the wealthiest students accumulate significant levels of educational debt to receive an advanced educational credential. According to data from the *Baccalaureate and Beyond 1993/1997* longitudinal survey, average educational debt in 1997 for dependent students who had not received an advanced degree was $13,626; however, dependent students who obtained a graduate or professional degree accumulated $27,453 in total educational debt.

Table 3.2 shows that total educational debt among students with advanced degrees varies considerably. For example, total educational debt for African Americans with an advanced degree was $23,882, on average, compared to $32,122 for Hispanics and $26,862 for whites. Similarly, low-income dependent students with a graduate or professional degree had almost $23,000 in total educational debt compared to $25,248 for lower-middle-income students, $31,768 for upper-middle-income students, and $32,322 for upper-income students. These averages suggest that students from low-income, lower-middle-income, and African American families are borrowing less money to obtain a post-

Table 3.2   Average Total Educational Debt ($) for 1992–1993 College Graduates with a Master's or First Professional Degree in 1997

All students	27,453
Type of undergraduate institution	
Research/doctoral	31,621
Comprehensive	21,804
Race and ethnicity	
White	26,682
African American	23,882
Hispanic	32,122
Economic class	
High-income	32,322
Upper-middle-income	31,768
Lower-middle-income	25,248
Low-income	22,720

Source: National Center for Education Statistics (2000a).

graduate degree than are high-income, upper-middle-income, and white students.

One reason that college graduates from disadvantaged positions within the social stratification system are incurring lower total educational debt to obtain an advanced degree is because they attended less expensive comprehensive undergraduate colleges and universities. In fact, comprehensive college graduates who received an advanced degree by 1997 had total educational debt of $21,804, on average, compared to a total educational debt of $31,621 for graduates of research and doctoral institutions.

Table 3.3 provides the linear regression estimates on total educational debt for dependent students who received a bachelor's degree in 1992–1993. The data confirm that economic class and gender characteristics of students are related to cumulative educational debt after controlling for educational attainment and the type of undergraduate institution attended. Among all students with educational debt in 1997, low-income students

Table 3.3   Linear Regression Estimates on Total Educational Debt in 1997 Among 1992–1993 College Graduates

Independent Variables	Beta Coefficient	Standard Error	T-statistic
Women	−3594.481	790.105	−4.55***
Hispanic	−126.782	1558.158	−0.08
African American	−865.194	1096.814	−0.79
Asian American	6264.086	3085.053	2.03*
Low-income	−2908.466	1460.400	−1.99*
Lower-middle-income	−4240.760	1500.583	−2.83**
Upper-middle-income	−1750.115	1567.523	−1.12
Had graduate degree in 1997	14564.950	1504.108	9.68***
Undergraduate institution was research/doctoral	−524.623	1062.109	−0.49
Undergraduate institution was comprehensive	−3744.494	1064.644	−3.52***
Constant	19058.260	1655.688	11.51***

Source: National Center for Education Statistics (2000a).
Notes: N = 378,599
R^2 = .1149
*** P < .001, ** P < .01, * P < .05

and lower-middle-income students borrowed between \$2,900 and \$4,200 less than high-income students. This model further shows that obtaining a graduate or professional degree increased total educational debt, on average, by \$14,565 for 1992–1993 college graduates. Among students who obtained a graduate or professional degree by 1997, women had, on average, \$5,721 less educational debt than men, whereas low-income and middle-income students had \$5,222 and \$5,724 less educational debt than high-income students. In addition, students who received an advanced degree by 1997 and borrowed as undergraduates had an additional \$18,573 in total educational debt (see Appendix C).

These models indicate that borrowing as an undergraduate adds considerably to the total educational debt necessary to obtain a graduate or professional degree. In addition, students from disadvantaged locations within the social system are borrowing less, on average, than more privileged students, in part because they attend less expensive comprehensive colleges and universities.

Labor Market Returns: Payoffs to the College Degree

The overreliance on student loans to pay for higher education appears to impact the initial college choices of lower-income and African American students. By attending less expensive comprehensive colleges and universities, rather than research or doctoral institutions, these students reduce their probability of obtaining a graduate or professional degree; if low-income and African American students are successful in earning an advanced degree, they incur considerably lower total educational debt. Even with this lower debt, however, lower-income students and racial and ethnic minorities face inequities due to lower salaries earned in the labor market.

Despite the substantially higher wages that workers with post-secondary credentials earn relative to workers with a high school education or less, significant differences in earnings remain between men and women, as well as among whites, African Americans, and Hispanics. Recent research documented that family socioeconomic background and college selectivity affect future earnings. One study (Thomas and Zhang 2001) found that college graduates from more affluent backgrounds enjoy greater returns to postsecondary education than do lower-income students, and first-generation college graduates have significantly lower returns than students whose parents have a college degree. One recent study (S. Thomas 2003) found that graduates from mid- and high-selective private colleges and universities had earnings 9 percent to 12 percent higher than those of graduates from low- and mid-selective public and private colleges. Graduates from liberal arts colleges had a significant earnings penalty (S. L. Thomas, 2003).

Salary Differences in 1997:
Impact of Family Background Characteristics,
Educational Attainment, and Type of College

In 1997, the average salary for 1992–1993 college graduates employed full-time was $33,721. Yet full-time workers from high-income backgrounds earned 14 percent more than workers from low-income backgrounds ($36,347 versus $31,946), and workers from upper-middle-income backgrounds earned 9 percent more than workers from low-income backgrounds. In fact, a clear linear correlation exists between economic class background and 1997 salaries among full-time workers. There was not a statistical difference in average salaries according to educational attainment: full-time workers with a graduate or professional degree earned $33,866, compared to $33,700 for workers without an advanced degree.

The type of undergraduate institution attended does affect average salaries: full-time workers in 1997 who received a bachelor's degree from a research or doctoral university had higher salaries, whereas workers who received a bachelor's degree from a comprehensive or liberal arts institution had lower salaries. Graduates of research and doctoral undergraduate institutions had average salaries of $35,724 in 1997, compared to $32,326 for comprehensive college and university graduates and $30,844 for liberal arts college graduates. Because low-income African American and Hispanic students disproportionately attend comprehensive colleges, it is reasonable to expect their 1997 salaries to be lower than college graduates from higher-income families and white students.

Table 3.4 shows that average 1997 salaries are different among students from different race, ethnic, economic class, and gender backgrounds. These differences illustrate the multidimensionality of income inequality among college graduates based on those characteristics. In every instance, men have higher salaries than women, regardless of economic class background, race, or ethnicity. For example, among full-time workers from high-income backgrounds, the average salary in 1997 for white men was $42,758, compared to $30,890 for white women. Similarly, African American men from high-income backgrounds earned more than $34,000, compared to $31,178 for African American women. And Hispanic men from high-income backgrounds earned $39,550, compared to $26,309 for Hispanic women. This pattern holds among men and women from low-income backgrounds as well.

Table 3.4   Average Annual Salaries ($) for 1992–1993 College Graduates Employed Full-Time and Not Enrolled, April 1997

	Men (37,965)	Women (30,220)
All workers (33,721)		
High-income (36,347)		
White	42,758	30,890
African American	34,040	31,178
Hispanic	39,550	26,309
Upper-middle-income (34,967)		
White	38,529	31,337
African American	36,322	34,507
Hispanic	43,366	33,339
Lower-middle-income (33,094)		
White	37,693	28,764
African American	35,573	28,034
Hispanic	39,083	32,028
Low-income (31,946)		
White	35,072	28,947
African American	32,935	28,405
Hispanic	34,100	25,653

Source: National Center for Education Statistics (2000a).

Average 1997 salaries for full-time white male workers from higher-income backgrounds were higher compared to those for African American male workers from higher-income backgrounds. White male workers received a salary premium of at least 6 percent in 1997 compared to African American male workers. Average salaries for white men from high-income backgrounds were 26 percent higher than African American men from high-income backgrounds, although very few black men in the sample were from high-income families. However, white male workers from low- and lower-middle-income backgrounds had lower average 1997 salaries than men in general. African American men from all economic class backgrounds had lower average 1997 salaries than men in general.

For women, the figures were different. White women from upper-income backgrounds generally earned 1 to 10 percent less than African American women from upper-income backgrounds. These salaries were still higher than salaries for women in general and were considerably lower than average 1997 salaries for men. In contrast, white women from lower-income backgrounds who worked full-time in 1997 earned about 3 percent more than African American women from lower-income backgrounds. With the exception of Hispanic women from lower-middle-income backgrounds, women from lower economic class backgrounds had lower salaries than all men and lower salaries than women in general.

Hispanic men who worked full-time in 1997 earned considerably higher salaries than Hispanic women, regardless of economic class background. However, the relationship between Hispanic and white men and women appears more complex. For example, Hispanic men and women from lower-middle-income and upper-middle-income backgrounds had higher average 1997 salaries than white men and women from similar economic class backgrounds. In contrast, Hispanic men and women from the highest and lowest economic class backgrounds had lower average 1997 salaries than white men and women from the same economic class backgrounds. One possible explanation is that many Hispanics attended research and doctoral universities, something that is associated with higher 1997 salaries (see Figure 3.3).

In sum, average salaries in 1997 are consistent with the contours of the unequal social system—a system of race, ethnic, gender, and class inequality:

1. College graduates from more affluent economic backgrounds have higher salaries than college graduates from lower economic class backgrounds;
2. Male college graduates have higher salaries than female college graduates; and
3. White college graduates have higher salaries than African American and Hispanic college graduates.

These patterns of income inequality contribute to the process of social reproduction that results from the overreliance on student loans to finance higher education.

The Emergent Process of Social Reproduction

Chapter 2 illustrated that the price of higher education continues to outpace inflation and that the financial aid available to help students and families pay higher prices increasingly comes in the form of loans. In the absence of sufficient grant financial aid, education loans certainly help students attend college, but loans also add considerably to the price of college because of accrued interest. In fact, borrowing for college *increases* the prices paid by students and their families, in contrast to grant aid, which *reduces* the price of college. In this chapter, evidence was presented to illustrate the impact of federal financial aid policy on decisions about going to college and about where to attend college.

Consistent with social reproduction theory, the overreliance on student loans to finance higher education imposes constraints on students from disadvantaged economic or race/ethnic positions within the social stratification system. That is, the fundamental starting point of the social reproduction process within higher education is the overreliance on educational loans to pay for college. Students from disadvantaged positions within the social stratification system (e.g., low-income, African American, and Hispanic students) generally have more financial need;

therefore, they make college choices under structural conditions (i.e., the need to borrow) that impose higher prices for college compared to the price of college for higher-income and white students.

Consequently, many students from disadvantageous positions within the social system make reasonable decisions to attend less expensive comprehensive colleges in order to reduce their cumulative undergraduate debt. This choice indicates the constraining function that borrowing has on college choices for students from disadvantaged positions within the social system—a limitation not present for more affluent students who borrow larger amounts of money to attend more expensive and often more prestigious colleges. Thus, an indirect result of the overreliance on student loans to pay for higher education is that low-income, African American, and Hispanic students limit their opportunities to obtain a graduate or professional degree because they attended comprehensive colleges and universities.

Despite the limitations that this overreliance on student loans places on disadvantaged students, a small but growing proportion of them are earning bachelor's and graduate or professional degrees. Once these students enter the labor market, historical inequities in salaries between men and women and among whites, African Americans, and Hispanics exacerbate the significant levels of debt most students accumulate to pay for higher education. Students from lower-income backgrounds, women, and African Americans earn considerably lower salaries in the labor market. These lower salaries, in conjunction with lower levels of educational attainment and the overreliance on student loans to pay for college, result in educational debt burden. In Chapter 4, the magnitude of educational debt burden is explored.

Notes

1. Appendix A lists the income quartiles used for this analysis; the income quartiles were created from an index measuring the ratio of student and family income as a proportion of the 1991 federal poverty thresholds and controls for family size.

2. The data for this study are from *Baccalaureate and Beyond Longitudinal Survey: 93/97* (1997), which is collected by the U.S. Department of Education's National Center for Education

Statistics. *Baccalaureate and Beyond* tracks a cohort of recent college graduates who received a bachelor's degree during the 1992–1993 academic year and who were first interviewed as part of the National Postsecondary Student Aid Survey (NPSAS). The NPSAS survey is a stratified multistage sample design with postsecondary institutions as the first-stage unit and students within institutions as the second-stage unit. Although sample weights are provided to allow the sample to reflect the national population of 1992–1993 bachelor's degree recipients (Green et al. 1999, 1996), the clustering technique of the sample design violates the "equal probability of selection" requirement necessary for valid statistical inferences. In order to control for the resulting bias in parameter estimates, I use the panel weight provided in the database and STATA complex survey software to generate robust standard errors that account for the stratified sample design. (For an empirical explanation of the need for this approach, see Thomas and Heck 2000).

Baccalaureate and Beyond data exist for 1994 and 1997. In 1994, 12,748 of the cases were identified from NPSAS as potential sample cases for *Baccalaureate and Beyond;* 10,958 of these cases were eligible and represented the population universe for the 1994 *Baccalaureate and Beyond* first follow-up. Of these eligible cases, 10,080 responded to telephone interviews or were visited by field researchers—representing a 92 percent response rate. Because the research question for this analysis focuses on the distribution of educational debt burden four years after college graduation, the *Baccalaureate and Beyond* panel cohort data that responded to the initial NPSAS survey and both *Baccalaureate and Beyond* follow-ups (1994 and 1997) are used. The panel sample represents 9,592 cases.

3. Millet (2003) and Heller (2001a) found no statistical effect of undergraduate debt on graduate enrollments. One explanation for these results is that financial aid awards for graduate school may be more important in the decisionmaking process than past debt for undergraduate study. Neither study cited above controlled for graduate financial aid packages.

4. Standard error bias resulting from the sample design was adjusted using STATA statistical software for complex survey samples.

5. See Appendix B for the logistic estimate tables.

4 The Educational Debt Burden Among College-Educated Workers

S tudents from high-income backgrounds and white students are less likely to need loans to pay for college. Even if these students do borrow for college, they use loans to attend more expensive research and doctoral universities that help them gain entry to graduate and professional programs and also lead to higher salaries in their early careers. And as Chapter 3 illustrated, low-income students and African American students tend to graduate from less expensive comprehensive colleges and universities in order to reduce their cumulative educational debt. Although those students, on average, have lower total educational debt, they are less likely to obtain an advanced degree and tend to receive lower salaries once they enter the labor market. These lower salaries result in higher educational debt burden.

Educational debt burden represents a new form of racial and economic class inequality. Students from low-income families are more likely to have excessive debt burden than students from higher-income families, and black students are more likely to have excessive debt burden than white students. That is to say, low-income students and black students who successfully attain a college degree are paying more for postsecondary education. Since educational loans require students to pay interest for ten years (assuming the standard term for loan repayment), the return on investment in higher education is lower for many borrowers. Moreover, the patterns of educational debt burden provide evidence of the regressive nature of the student aid system. Thus, student loans place an additional burden on low-income students and

71

black students who successfully pursue postsecondary education—
a burden that upper-income students and more affluent white students do not face.

What Is Educational Debt Burden?

Educational debt burden is measured by the ratio of monthly student loan payments to gross monthly income. According to the
U.S. Department of Education as well as loan industry analysts,
students who exceed an 8 percent threshold of educational debt to
monthly income are at greater risk of student loan default and
other economic hardships. Loan defaults increase the cost of the
federal student loan programs because the government guarantees
student loans and therefore pays the lender the full value of
defaulted loans. Loan defaults also impact the ability of colleges
and universities to participate in federal student aid programs.
Since 1992, colleges and universities with cohort loan default
rates higher than 15 percent are excluded from participating in
federal financial aid programs authorized in Title IV of the Higher
Education Act. Finally, students who default on federal loans can
no longer participate in federal student aid programs, which can
have serious consequences, especially for students who did not
complete a postsecondary education.

The Trend in Student Debt Levels

Given the dramatic change in student financial aid policy and the
increasingly important role of a bachelor's degree, more college
students are borrowing more money to help pay for college. The
steady increase in student borrowing in the federal Stafford Loan
program, after cumulative loan limits were increased by the 1992
reauthorization of the Higher Education Act, resulted in higher
total educational debt for undergraduates as well as graduate students. One reason for the increase is that loans were used by students to pay for 95 percent of the increased charges at public four-
year colleges between 1991 and 1995 and to pay for 65 percent of
the increased charges between 1995 and 1999 (Lumina
Foundation 2002). Between 1995 and 1998, cumulative loan balances increased 15 percent for undergraduates and doubled for
graduate students (Scherschel 1998). By 1999, the share of "heav-

ily indebted" undergraduates rose to 40 percent (Scherschel 2000).[1] According to the National Postsecondary Student Aid Survey, average undergraduate educational debt levels for college graduates exceeded $18,000 in 2000.

This increased reliance on student loans to pay for college is causing concern among some federal policymakers, advocacy organizations, and higher education policy analysts (see *Slamming Shut the Doors to College* 2002; King and Bannon 2002; National Center for Public Policy and Higher Education 2002). One study (King and Bannon 2002) found that 64 percent of students graduated with loan debt in 1999–2000 and that average debt more than doubled compared to 1992. More than 70 percent of students from families with incomes less than $20,000 graduated with some level of debt in 1999–2000, compared to 44 percent of students from families with incomes greater than $100,000 (King and Bannon 2002).

Rising student debt levels have implications for students' success in college and for their continuing education and career decisions. For example, students with higher debt levels are less likely to continue beyond the first or second year at both public and private colleges (Cofer and Somers 2000, 1999). A 1997 survey of student borrowers found that 70 percent of black, Hispanic, and Asian borrowers who did *not* complete a degree said that loans had prevented them from staying in school (Baum and Saunders 1998). For those who finished their degree program, 40 percent of students with debt delayed purchasing a home, 31 percent delayed purchasing a car, and 22 percent delayed having children (Baum and Saunders 1998). A 2002 survey of student borrowers found that 41 percent of low-income borrowers felt loans limited their college choices, and 39 percent of low-income borrowers responded that loan repayments caused more hardship than anticipated (Baum and O'Malley 2003). Similarly, among different race and ethnic groups, a larger proportion of black (44 percent) and Hispanic (51 percent) borrowers felt loans limited their college choices compared to white (35 percent) borrowers (Baum and O'Malley 2003).

Educational Debt Burden One Year After Graduation

Although the lifetime payoff to a college education is considerable, salaries in early careers are much lower than national averages imply. The U.S. Census reported that 1994 average annual income for people twenty-five years and older with a college degree was $56,298 for men and $30,568 for women.[2] Yet average salaries in the early careers of college graduates in *Baccalaureate and Beyond 1993/1997* were only $21,154 for men and $21,036 for women. These low salaries can result in high educational debt burden.

Figure 4.1 illustrates that about one in six 1992–1993 college graduates who were working and not enrolled in graduate school had educational debt burden greater than 8 percent one year after receiving a bachelor's degree. Undergraduate educational debt levels are not significantly different for students with high or moderate debt burden; however, college graduates with debt burden greater than 8 percent had significantly lower salaries than other college graduates. Average 1994 salaries for workers with excessive debt burden was $16,363 compared to $20,152 for workers without educational debt burden and $25,026 for workers with educational debt burden less than 8 percent.

Educational Debt Burden Four Years After College

In 1997, according to the National Center for Education Statistics, median educational debt burden for students employed full-time

Figure 4.1   Educational Debt Burden in 1994 Among College Graduates

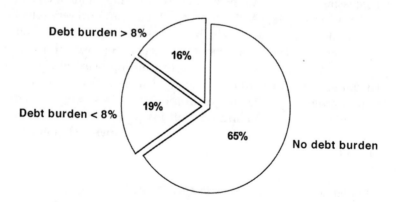

Source: National Center for Education Statistics (2000a).

in 1997 was less than 5 percent; however, 17 percent of those students had debt burden greater than 10 percent (National Center for Education Statistics 2000c). One study (Heller 2001a) found loan balances declined, on average, between 1994 and 1997 for students who did not enroll in graduate school. Yet the rate of declining balances was much slower for African Americans and lower-income students. In 1997, for African Americans, 49 percent of their undergraduate loan balance was outstanding, compared to 37 percent for whites. For lower-income students, 46 percent of their undergraduate loan balance was outstanding in 1997, compared to 31 percent and 25 percent for upper-middle-income and upper-income college graduates (Heller 2001a).

Figure 4.2 illustrates the distribution of educational debt burden in 1997 among full-time workers not enrolled in a graduate or professional degree program. A smaller proportion of college graduates had educational debt burden greater than 8 percent in 1997 (11.3 percent) than in 1994 (15.6 percent), but a larger proportion had some level of educational debt burden in 1997 (37 percent) than in 1994 (35 percent). One reason that a larger proportion of 1992–1993 college graduates had educational debt burden in 1997 is that fewer students were enrolled in a graduate or professional degree program, and many students had obtained an advanced degree.

Figure 4.2   **Educational Debt Burden in 1997 Among College Graduates**

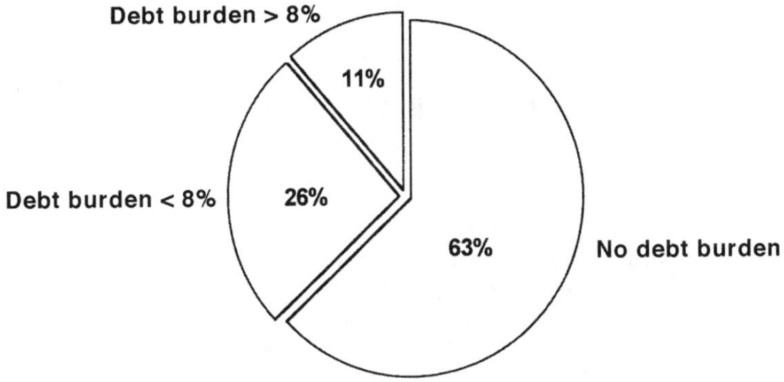

Source: National Center for Education Statistics (2000a).

Average salaries in 1997 were considerably higher than in 1994, increasing 65 percent to $33,721. As Chapter 3 illustrated, there was not a statistical difference between average salaries of workers with an advanced degree and workers with only a bachelor's degree; however, full-time workers with educational debt burden greater than 8 percent had considerably lower salaries than other workers. Table 4.1 shows that salaries among 1992–1993 college graduates with excessive debt burden were about $26,300, which is 28 percent lower than the average salary for all workers in 1997. Clearly, inequities in labor market salaries impact educational debt burden in early careers.

The level of debt that students accumulate can also influence educational debt burden. Average debt in 1997 for full-time workers not enrolled in graduate or professional school was almost $13,000. But workers with an advanced degree had almost twice as much total educational debt in 1997 ($22,633). Workers with debt burden greater than 8 percent also had much larger average educational debt ($22,496) than did other full-time workers. Thus, total cumulative debt can also impact educational debt burden in early careers.

Predicting 1997 Educational Debt Burden

The *Baccalaureate and Beyond 1993/1997* longitudinal survey can be used to test for the existence of race, ethnic, gender, and income inequality measured by educational debt burden.[3] Does

Table 4.1   Average 1997 Salaries ($) Among Full-Time Workers Who Graduated from College in 1992–1993

All workers	33,721
Workers with a graduate or professional degree	33,866
Workers with bachelor's degree only	33,700
Workers with educational debt burden > 8%	26,321
Workers with educational debt burden < 8%	36,199
Workers without educational debt burden	34,041

Source: National Center for Education Statistics (2000a).

educational attainment explain why some students have excessive debt burden? Or are patterns of educational debt burden consistent with the social system of race, ethnic, gender, and economic class inequality? A sophisticated statistical technique—multinomial logistic regression—is a helpful tool to help explain differences in educational debt burden in 1997. The multinomial model is basically an extended logit that simultaneously estimates the effects for a given set of outcomes compared to a particular reference category (Long 1997). The multinomial estimates allow for statistical inferences controlling for other variables in the model. For example, relative risk ratios and their directionality (e.g., greater than 1 is positive, less than 1 is negative) provide a means to interpret the empirical results. Subsequently, comparisons can be made among the relative effects of family background characteristics, educational attainment, and occupational fields on educational debt burden in 1997.

Occupations and College Majors

Because salaries vary among occupations, control variables were created for occupational field of employment in 1997 (legal, medical, K-12 education, non–K-12 education, professional, management, computer/technical, and support services). The reference category for 1997 occupation was sales and trades. Undergraduate and graduate field of study may also influence debt burden; thus, control variables were created for the undergraduate fields of business, engineering, education, health, social sciences, biology, and math, and for the graduate fields of social sciences and humanities, engineering and science, medicine and law, education, and business management. The reference category was "other." Additional variables included in the statistical model represent standard demographic measures for race, ethnicity, gender, and income as well as nondemographic factors that may influence educational debt burden, such as undergraduate institutional control and educational attainment.

The data were limited by excluding those students who did not borrow for their undergraduate or graduate education. This step reduced the sample size to 4,485 cases and introduced bias into the model estimates. However, graduates without debt burden are disproportionately from higher-income families who did not qualify for federal loans under the 1992 need-analysis formula. In addition, the unsubsidized Stafford Loan was not widely available prior to 1993. Thus, the effect sizes from this model are rather conservative and represent lower bound estimates.[4]

Educational debt burden is measured as the proportion of monthly income used to service student loans. The dependent variable measures three categories of educational debt burden in 1997: (1) educational debt burden is greater than or equal to 8 percent; (2) educational debt burden is greater than zero but less than 8 percent; and (3) educational debt burden was greater than zero in 1994 and declined to zero in 1997.[5] This measure of educational debt burden included students with monthly loan payments greater than or equal to zero and salaries greater than or equal to zero. Missing cases were reduced by setting cases that had missing 1994 salary data, but did not have a loan payment, to zero 1994 debt burden.[6] Debt burden ratios greater than 100 percent of income were reset to 1. In the *Baccalaureate and Beyond* sample, the variable provided to measure total monthly educational debt payments excludes student loans in deferment or sets them to zero. Because loan deferment is a strategy used by many borrowers with high debt levels, educational debt burden may be underestimated.[7]

Descriptive Results

Among college graduates with educational debt, debt burden declined to zero for 38 percent of students between 1994 and 1997. In 1997, 41 percent of students had educational debt burden less than 8 percent; for 21 percent of students educational debt burden was greater than or equal to 8 percent (see Figure 4.3). Debt burden can vary because of the amount borrowed for college and because of the level of current salary. Average debt in 1997 for all students in the subsample was $15,355, but for students with debt burden greater than 8 percent, average debt was more than $23,000. Similarly, average salary in 1997 for all students was $31,556, but for students with educational debt burden greater than 8 percent, average salary was less than $24,000. For all students with educational debt burden greater than 8 percent,

Figure 4.3   Educational Debt Burden in 1997 Among Workers Who Borrowed for College

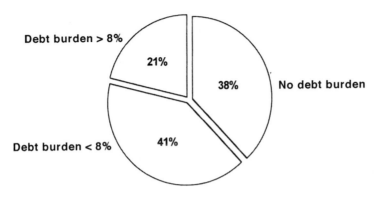

Source: National Center for Education Statistics (2000a).

average debt was significantly higher and average salaries were significantly lower. This pattern is true regardless of race, ethnic, economic class, or gender characteristics.

Table 4.2 shows that educational debt burden in 1997 varies among workers by race, ethnic, gender, and economic class backgrounds. Lower-income students were overrepresented among students whose debt burden exceeded the 8 percent threshold: 26 percent of students from low-income families had debt burden greater than 8 percent, compared to 21 percent of all students. Similarly, 48 percent of students from low-income families and 43 percent of students from lower-middle-income families had educational debt burden less than 8 percent, compared to 41 percent of all students. In contrast, 63 percent of students from high-income families and 46 percent of students from upper-middle-income families saw their educational debt burden decline to zero between 1994 and 1997; only 26 percent of students from low-income families had educational debt burden decline to zero during this period.

Women, African Americans, and Hispanics were also overrepresented among students with debt burden above the 8 percent threshold. Slightly more than 23 percent of women had educational debt burden greater than 8 percent in 1997, 28 percent of

Table 4.2 Distribution of Educational Debt Burden in 1997 by Race, Ethnicity, Gender, and Economic Class Background (percentage)

Variable	Declined to Zero	Less Than 8%	Greater Than or Equal to 8%
Economic class			
Low-income***	26.20	47.80	25.90
Lower-middle-income	35.70	43.10	21.20
Upper-middle-income***	46.20	35.20	18.60
Upper-income***	62.60	24.30	13.00
Race and ethnicity			
White	38.50	40.40	21.00
Asian***	53.40	27.40	19.20
Black**	28.90	47.10	24.10
Hispanic***	23.20	49.30	27.50
Gender			
Men			
Women**	37.50	39.30	23.20
All students	37.80	40.80	21.40

Source: National Center for Education Statistics (2000a).
Notes: N = 4485
*** P < .001, ** P < .01

Hispanics had educational debt burden greater than 8 percent in 1997, and 24 percent of African Americans had educational debt burden greater than 8 percent in 1997; these proportions are significantly higher than the 21 percent of all students with debt burden greater than 8 percent in 1997. In contrast, 39 percent of whites saw debt burden decline to zero between 1994 and 1997, but educational debt burden declined to zero for only 23 percent of Hispanics and 29 percent of African Americans during that period.

The statistical relationship between race, ethnicity, gender, and income compounds these patterns (see Figure 4.4). Blacks and Hispanics are disproportionately represented among students from low-income backgrounds; 58 percent of Hispanics and 49 percent of blacks were from low-income families, compared to 38 percent of all students. Blacks and Hispanics are also underrepresented among higher income groups. Only 3 percent of blacks were from

Figure 4.4   Distribution of Economic Class Backgrounds by Race, Ethnicity, and Gender

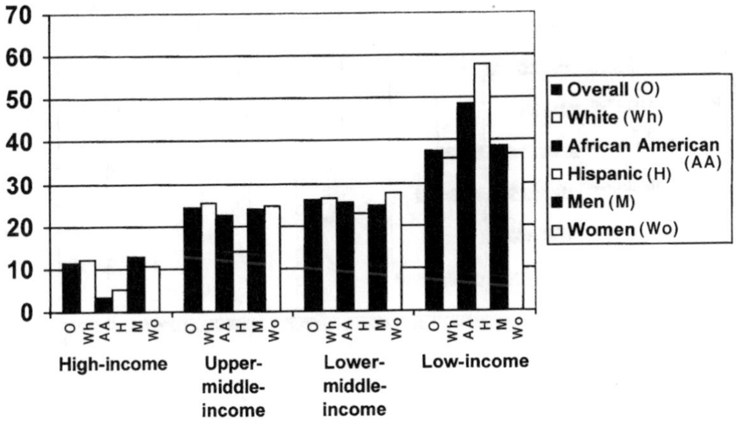

Source: National Center for Education Statistics (2000a).

high-income families, and 22 percent were from upper-middle-income backgrounds, compared to 11 percent of all students who are from high-income backgrounds and 24 percent who are from upper-middle-income families. Women are also underrepresented among students from high-income families. Conversely, more than 12 percent of whites were from high-income backgrounds and 26 percent were from upper-middle-income families, but whites were underrepresented among students from low-income families (36 percent versus 38 percent overall). Simply put, black and Hispanic students are disproportionately from low-income families, whereas high-income students are disproportionately white.

Multinomial Logit Results

Figure 4.5 illustrates the relative risk ratios for workers with educational debt burden greater than 8 percent in 1997 for different race, ethnic, gender, and economic class backgrounds (see Appendix D for tables). The results indicate strong effects of race and economic class background on educational debt burden exceeding the 8 percent threshold in 1997, four years after receiving the baccalaureate degree. These effects hold even after con-

Figure 4.5   Relative Risk Ratios of Educational Debt Burden Exceeding 8 Percent in 1997 Among 1992–1993 College Graduates

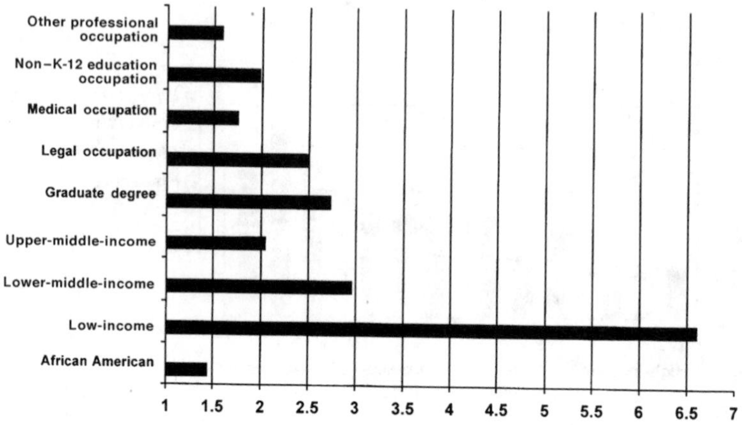

Source: National Center for Education Statistics (2000a).

trolling for the undergraduate and graduate field of study, graduation from a public undergraduate institution, graduate or professional degree attainment, and 1997 occupation.

The effect of being from a low-income, lower-middle-income, or upper-middle-income family on the 8 percent threshold was positive and significant. Students from low-income families were 6.5 times more likely than upper-income students to have educational debt burden exceeding the 8 percent threshold in 1997. The relative risk ratio for lower-middle-income students was 2.95, and for upper-middle-income students it was 2.05. Thus, all but the highest-income students were more likely to have educational debt burden exceeding 8 percent compared to debt burden declining to zero between 1994 and 1997. Moreover, African Americans were 1.4 times more likely than whites to have excessive educational debt burden in 1997.

The effect of postgraduate degree attainment on the 8 percent threshold was also positive and significant: students who attained a master's or first professional degree by 1997 were 2.7 times more likely than students with only a bachelor's degree to have educational debt burden exceed 8 percent. Although students who graduated from comprehensive undergraduate colleges and universities accumulated lower total educational debts than graduates of research and doctoral institutions, receiving a bachelor's degree from a comprehensive college was not statistically significant. The effects of the undergraduate and graduate field of study on the 8 percent threshold were generally not statistically significant. However, as one would expect, workers in the medical, legal, non–K-12 education, and other professional occupations were more likely to have educational debt burden exceed 8 percent.

Given the disproportionate number of low-income families from Hispanic backgrounds (see Figure 4.4), a linear interaction effect of income and ethnicity on educational debt burden being greater than 8 percent was tested. These interactions indicate that low-income Hispanics had 8.3 times greater risk than did white students with higher incomes. This linear interaction was statistically significant (P = .001), which suggests that the effect of ethnicity on educational debt burden exceeding 8 percent for Hispanics is embedded in the income measure of economic class background.

Explaining Educational Debt Burden in 1997

The effect of having a low-income, lower-middle-income, and upper-middle-income background on educational debt burden was expected. Students from families with lower incomes have fewer resources to pay for college, and the buying power of need-based grants has declined over the past two decades. Consequently, these students must rely on loans to help pay for college, which increases their educational debt burden. In contrast, upper-income families do not often qualify for need-based grant aid. Although students with educational debt burden greater than 8 percent borrowed significantly more than all students in 1997, students from lower-income families, on average, borrowed less than students from higher-income families. And average salaries in 1997 for lower-income students were significantly less than for high-income students (see Table 3.4). College graduates from higher-income families earned 14 percent more than college graduates from lower-income families in 1997. These data suggest that low-income and lower-middle-income students had high debt burden because of lower salaries, whereas upper-middle-income students had high debt burden because of more borrowing.

The effect of race on educational debt burden is telling, because African Americans are disproportionately from low-income backgrounds. That is to say, even after controlling for family income, being African American had an independent effect on educational debt burden in 1997. Since African Americans are attending less expensive comprehensive colleges, in part to reduce the amount borrowed to pay for college, African Americans' debt burden is more a function of race differentials in occupational salaries. Descriptive data show that average salaries among African Americans with educational debt burden greater than 8 percent are considerably lower than for whites overall. African Americans with educational debt burden greater than 8 percent had average salaries of $25,789 in 1997 compared to average salaries of $31,256 for all whites. Moreover, average debt for African Americans with excessive educational debt burden is also significantly higher than for whites. In 1997, the average for African Americans with high educational debt burden was more than $20,000 compared to $15,416 for all whites (see Table 4.3).

The effect of ethnicity (e.g., the Hispanic population) on educational debt burden was not statistically significant in the model. Several possibilities for this nonsignificant effect come to mind: receiving a bachelor's degree from a research or doctoral university, earning a postgraduate degree by 1997, or choice of occupational field could explain the disproportionate numbers of Hispanics whose educational debt burden exceeds the 8 percent threshold. However, the linear interaction effect between low income and Hispanic indicates an increased risk for low-income Hispanics to exceed the 8 percent threshold. Therefore, an alternative explanation for the nonsignificant effects of ethnicity in the multinomial model is that 58 percent of Hispanics are from low-income families, and the low-income measure better captures the uniform effect of class on educational debt burden independent of ethnic status. In other words, the effect of being Hispanic on educational debt burden exceeding 8 percent is not readily separated from the effect of being from a low-income family.

Educational Debt Burden and Social Inequality

College graduates with debt burden exceeding 8 percent face financial hardships in their early careers. Among students with

Table 4.3   **Average Debt and Average Salary in 1997 for All Students and for Students with Debt Burden Greater Than 8 Percent**

	Average Debt		Average Salary	
Variable	All Students ($)	Debt Burden > 8% ($)	All Students ($)	Debt Burden > 8% ($)
Race and ethnicity				
White	15,416	23,087	31,256	23,368
Black	14,236	20,023	31,593	25,789
Hispanic	13,424	21,206	31,319	24,325
Asian	21,782	33,478	39,134	31,323
Economic class				
Low-income	14,422	20,293	30,391	23,707
Lower-middle-income	14,709	22,157	31,108	21,333
Upper-middle-income	17,042	26,481	32,794	26,065
Upper-income	18,743	33,486	34,134	27,020
Gender				
Men	16,445	26,260	35,681	26,302
Women	14,520	20,956	28,374	22,233
Overall	15,355	23,025	31,556	23,795

Source: National Center for Education Statistics (2000a).

educational loans, more than one in five college graduates had excessive educational debt burden four years after receiving a bachelor's degree. These students have higher educational debt and lower salaries than typical college graduates: in 1997, average debt for students with high educational debt burden was more than $23,000 while average salary was about $23,800 (see Table 4.3). Postgraduate degree attainment does not explain why these students have debt burden that exceeds the 8 percent threshold. Rather, college graduates with high debt burden are disproportionately from families with incomes less than six times poverty and are especially likely to be from low-income families (with incomes less than 1.85 times poverty). They are also more likely to be African American.

The financial hardship of educational debt burden can be especially difficult given the ongoing salary inequities in the labor market between workers from disadvantageous positions within the social system and workers from more privileged backgrounds. Low-income students, African Americans, and Hispanics are more likely to choose less expensive comprehensive colleges and universities to avoid large amounts of educational debt. Even so, they are more likely to face excessive educational debt burden once they enter the labor market. Students from lower-income families are more likely to have excessive debt burden compared to students from higher-income families, and black students are more likely to have excessive debt burden compared to white students. Thus, in terms of educational debt burden, the overreliance on student loans to pay for college reinforces the race, ethnic, and economic class system of American society.

Notes

1. "Heavily indebted" was defined as students with cumulative loan balances greater than $10,000.

2. See www.census.gov/hhes/income/histinc/p18.html.

3. See Chapter 3 for details about *Baccalaureate and Beyond*. Educational debt burden is also addressed in my forthcoming article, "Educational Debt Burden Among Student Borrowers: An Analysis of the Baccalaureate and Beyond Panel, 1997 Follow-up," *Research in Higher Education* 45(7), November 2004.

4. About 47 percent of college graduates responding to the survey reported zero educational debt burdens in both 1994 and 1997; these students were excluded from the analysis. The following table shows that these students were disproportionately from higher-income families.

Family Income in 1991*	Proportion Without Educational Debt Burden (percentage) (N = 4037)
Low-income	39.6
Lower-middle-income	44.1
Upper-middle-income	51.3
Upper-income	61.8
Total	47.4

Note: * P = .001

5. Using a standard debt estimation model (Salary / 12 * .08) to represent the maximum monthly debt and a monthly payment estimator assuming a standard ten-year debt repayment schedule at 7 percent interest (Debt / $1000 * 12.25), I calculate a significantly different distribution of educational debt burden. By this measure in 1994, 45 percent of college graduates had zero debt burden, 31 percent had debt burden less than 8 percent, and 24 percent had debt burden greater than 8 percent. Similarly, in 1997 41 percent of college graduates had zero debt burden, 41 percent had debt burden less than 8 percent, and 17 percent had debt burden greater than 8 percent. Simply put, this alternative measure of debt burden suggests that 55 percent of college graduates had debt burden one year after receiving a bachelor's degree, and 59 percent of college graduates had debt burden four years later. These proportions are significantly higher than the official data reported by the U.S. Department of Education.

6. A total of 406 cases had missing data in the multinomial model. These missing cases were correlated with the dependent variable (.221) and were disproportionately low-income students. The table below provides the demographic characteristics of the missing cases and reinforces that the model may be underestimating the demographic effects on changes in educational debt burden between 1994 and 1997.

Demographic Characteristics	Percentage of Missing Cases (N = 406)
Low-income	46.8
Lower-middle-income	23.9
Upper-middle-income	21.9
Upper-income	7.4
Men	46.1
Women	53.9
White	81.8
Asian	3.0
Black	5.2
Hispanic	8.4

7. There are two populations whose deferment and graduate enrollment status changes could affect the parameter estimates of educational burden in 1997. First, 230 students in deferment in 1994 were coded as having zero debt burden in 1994. Descriptive

data show that these students had educational debt burden in 1997 because they were no longer in deferment: 29 percent had debt burden more than 8 percent, and 71 percent had debt burden less than 8 percent. Second, 140 students who had debt burden in 1994 were coded with zero debt burden in 1997 due to graduate enrollment status and lack of 1997 salary. These cases entered the model in 1997 with debt burden declining to zero.

5 Educational Debt and Economic Class Reproduction

Almost thirty years ago, economists Samuel Bowles and Herbert Gintis published *Schooling in Capitalist America* (1976), in which they argued that schools were not intended to enable social mobility for students; rather, schools functioned to reinforce or reproduce the existing economic class structure of society. As evidence, Bowles and Gintis documented the "correspondence principle" that showed the likelihood that students from lower-class backgrounds would remain in disadvantaged economic positions as adults and that students from higher-class backgrounds would obtain equal or greater standing as adults. That is, students from different class backgrounds were sorted by the U.S. educational system into social and economic strata that corresponded with their family background.

In a recent article in *Sociology of Education,* Bowles and Gintis (2002) revisited their basic arguments to show empirically how other researchers validated their data. For example, one study (Hertz 2001) found that a male born in a family with income in the top decile has a one in five chance of achieving the top income decile. Conversely, a male born in a family with income in the poorest decile has only a one in 100 chance of achieving the top income decile and has a one in five chance of remaining in the poorest decile. An unrelated study (Karen 2002) found persistent direct effects of family income, race, and gender on college enrollments, even after controlling for academic factors. Because inequities in college access according to the ascriptive characteristics of students remain, this undermines the argument that schools equalize opportunities for people of color, women, and those from low-income families.

In 1979, the sociologist Randall Collins described the social reproduction of inequality in more cultural terms. He argued that the process of credential inflation represented the mechanism through which the most class-privileged students were able to reinforce their socioeconomic advantages. As explained in Chapter 3, the credential society reinforces the comparative advantage of class-privileged individuals because upper-class students are more successful in getting higher education credentials than their lower-class counterparts despite equal precollege aspirations, self-image, and college grades. This process raises concerns that the expansion of opportunities in higher education has produced a credential society where the pursuit of the college degree is more important than the substantive characteristics of learning (Labaree 1997). Moreover, a credential society emphasizes higher education as a private good, with the college degree representing a competitive advantage for some people over others.

Yet the value of higher education in economic terms does not positively accrue to all its graduates. A higher education credential may change the kinds of choices people have, but it does not guarantee upward mobility, job security, or a "middle-class" lifestyle (Carnoy 1974). In fact, the evidence provided in the previous chapters suggests that the overreliance on student loans to finance higher education reinforces social inequality because the need to borrow for college causes low-income students, African Americans, and Hispanics to choose less expensive comprehensive colleges, not to apply or enroll in graduate school, and not to obtain an advanced educational degree. Moreover, the overreliance on loans results in significantly higher educational debt burden for college graduates from low economic class backgrounds and from African American families. In this chapter, data from the *Baccalaureate and Beyond 1993/1997* longitudinal survey is examined to test for the relationship between students' economic class background and their household economic circumstances four years after receiving a bachelor's degree.

Measuring Economic Class Using a Poverty Index

Each year, the U.S. Census releases data that set the official poverty thresholds for families of various sizes. These thresholds are income ceilings based on the number of adults and dependent children in a family and are used to establish eligibility for many federal and state social welfare programs, such as food stamps, Medicare, Medicaid, and subsidized housing. A U.S. Department of Agriculture statistician, Molly Orshansky, established the formula for the official poverty threshold, known as the "Orshansky Model," in the mid-1950s. It measures the minimum amount of income necessary for a family to afford basic living expenses and a temporary emergency food diet. In the 1950s, basic food items required approximately one-third of a family's monthly income. Even today, the formula for the official poverty threshold is three times the temporary emergency food diet.

Figure 5.1 illustrates the distribution of economic class backgrounds for 1992–1993 college graduates based on their

Figure 5.1   Economic Class Backgrounds of 1992–1993 College Graduates

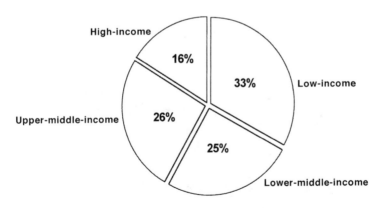

Source: National Center for Education Statistics (2000a).

Notes: Low: family income less than 1.85 times poverty; Lower-middle: family income between 1.85–3.4x poverty; Upper-middle: family income between 3.4–6x poverty; High: family income greater than 6x poverty.

See Appendix A.

1991 family income. Four discrete classes were created based
on the distribution of 1991 family income as a ratio of the official poverty threshold in that year. The low-income threshold
was set at 1.85 times poverty because that threshold is used to
determine eligibility for many social welfare programs. The
lower-middle-income category represents families with incomes
up to the median for the sample. The upper-middle-income category represents families with incomes greater than the median
but less than six times poverty. The high-income category represents students from families with income greater than six times
poverty. Based on 1991 family income data, 33 percent of
1992–1993 college graduates were from low-income backgrounds. About 25 percent of 1992–1993 college graduates
were from families with incomes between 1.85 and 3.4 times
poverty; 26 percent were from families with incomes between
3.4 and 6 times poverty; and 16 percent were from high-income
families.

Figure 5.2 shows that this economic class measure varies

**Figure 5.2   Economic Class Backgrounds of 1992–1993 College Graduates
by Race and Ethnicity (percentages)**

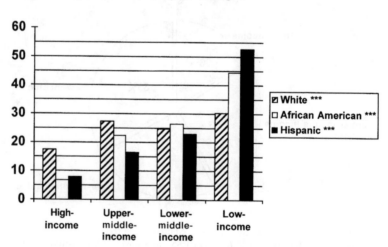

Source: National Center for Education Statistics (2000a).
Note: *** P < .001

significantly by the race and ethnic characteristics of the student. White students are overrepresented among high-income families, whereas African American, Hispanic, and female students are overrepresented among low-income families. For example, 18 percent of white college graduates were from high-income families compared to 16 percent of all students, 8 percent of Hispanics, and 7 percent of African Americans. In contrast, 44 percent of African American college graduates and 58 percent of Hispanic college graduates were from low-income families compared to one-third of all students and 30 percent of whites.

Household Income in 1997

Most students attend college in order to improve their socioeconomic circumstances. Several factors could impact household income for recent college graduates. For example, a recent college graduate may or may not be married, may or may not have children, and probably has considerable educational debt. In addition, the race and ethnic background of a student also influences salaries in early careers (see Table 3.4). African Americans and most Hispanics earn considerably less than whites. Figure 5.3 illustrates the differences in 1997 household income among college graduates by marital status and race and ethnicity.

Among all students working full-time in 1997, average household income was $44,396. Married households earned significantly more than single households ($58,210 versus $30,662) in part because 37 percent of college graduates who were married or committed to a "marriage-like" relationship had two incomes per household. Among married households, significant income differences were present between African Americans, Hispanics, and whites. In 1997, average income among white households was $58,574 compared to $53,184 for African Americans and $54,709 for Hispanics. Average household incomes for unmarried 1992–1993 college graduates did not differ significantly according to race or ethnic characteristics, ranging from $29,602 for African Americans to $29,803 for Hispanics and $30,061 for whites.

Figure 5.3   1997 Household Income ($) by Marital Status, Race, and
Ethnicity, 1992–1993 College Graduates

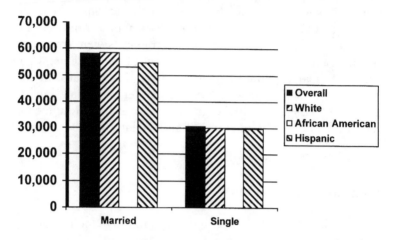

Source: National Center for Education Statistics (2000a).

Household Educational Debt

In 1997, educational debt for married households was almost
$2,000 higher than debt for single college graduates, in part
because 10 percent of spouses had at least a college degree and
15 percent reported some educational debt (see Figure 5.4).
Average household educational debt was not statistically significant between African American and white married households, and Hispanic married households had considerably
lower educational debt than white households ($13,879 versus
$17,509). In contrast, among single college graduates, African
Americans and Hispanics had significantly lower educational
debt than their white peers. Average educational debt for single
households in 1997 was $15,634, but both African American
and Hispanic households had less than $13,500 in educational
debt compared to $15,842 for white single households. As dis-
cussed in Chapter 3, these lower educational debts are in part
due to African Americans and Hispanics choosing less expensive comprehensive undergraduate colleges and universities,
and also because African Americans and Hispanics have lower

Figure 5.4   Average Household Educational Debt ($) in 1997 by Marital Status, Race, and Ethnicity, 1992–1993 College Graduates

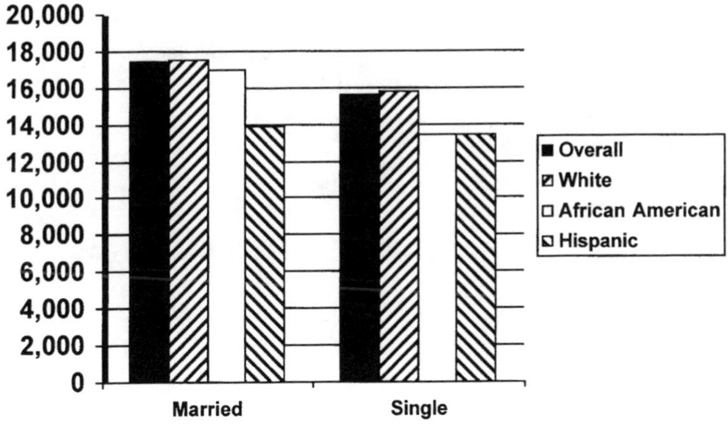

Source: National Center for Education Statistics (2000a).

overall educational attainment levels (i.e., fewer racial and ethnic minorities had a graduate or professional degree in 1997).

Household Educational Debt Burden in 1997

As Chapter 4 illustrated, among 1992–1993 college graduates, those from lower-income and African American families are much more likely to have excessive educational debt burden four years after receiving a bachelor's degree. Household educational debt burden in 1997 can also be estimated by calculating the maximum monthly debt payment that exceeds 8 percent of household income. Figure 5.5 illustrates that almost two-thirds of households had educational debt burden in 1997, and about 18 percent of households had educational debt burden exceeding 8 percent.

Figure 5.6 shows that households with excessive educational debt burden in 1997 are disproportionately African American and disproportionately from low-income family backgrounds. That is,

Figure 5.5   Distribution of 1997 Household Educational Debt Burden, 1992–1993 College Graduates

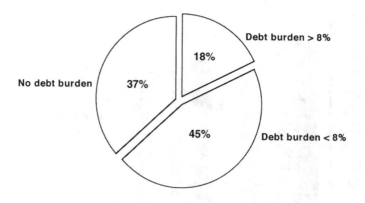

Source: National Center for Education Statistics (2000a).

Figure 5.6   Excessive Household Educational Debt Burden (> 8%) by Race, Ethnicity, and Economic Class Background in 1997, 1992–1993 College Graduates (percentages)

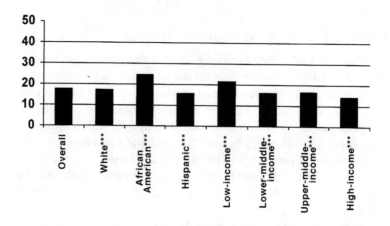

Source: National Center for Education Statistics (2000a).
Note: *** P < .001

almost 25 percent of African American households exceeded the 8 percent threshold in 1997, and 21 percent of households from low economic class backgrounds exceeded the threshold. In contrast, less than 16 percent of Hispanic households and only 14 percent of households from high-income backgrounds exceeded the 8 percent threshold.

One reason for high educational debt burden is lower household incomes. Among households with educational debt burden greater than 8 percent, household income was slightly more than $27,000. Households with educational debt burden less than 8 percent had an average income in 1997 of more than $50,000, and households without educational debt burden had an average income of almost $45,000. A second reason for high educational debt burden is higher educational debt. Among households with educational debt burden greater than 8 percent, average household educational debt was almost $34,000 compared to less than $10,000 among households with educational debt burden less than 8 percent (see Table 5.1).

Reproducing Economic Class Inequality Among College Graduates

One way to test the "correspondence principle" among college graduates is to compare poverty indices between 1991 and 1997 among 1992–1993 college graduates in the *Baccalaureate and Beyond 1993/1997* sample. Household income, marital status,

Table 5.1   Average Household Income and Educational Debt by Debt Burden Categories in 1997, 1992–1993 College Graduates

	Household Income ($)	Household Educational Debt ($)
Debt burden > 8%	27,190	33,957
Debt burden < 8%	50,056	9,857
Zero debt burden	44,824	N/A

Source: National Center for Education Statistics (2000a).
Note: N/A = not applicable.

and family size were used to calculate the ratio of 1997 household income to the official poverty thresholds. Figure 5.7 illustrates the distribution of household income among four discrete categories. About 12 percent of college graduates had low incomes in 1997 (less than 1.85 times poverty); 38 percent had a household income between 1.85 and 3.72 times poverty; 34 percent had a household income between 3.72 and 6 times poverty; and 17 percent had a household income greater than 6 times poverty. The median poverty index in 1997 for these students was 3.72, or 28 percent higher than the median poverty index in 1991. Moreover, the lowest quartile (25 percent) of households in 1997 had an income up to 2.6 times poverty compared to a ceiling of 1.39 times poverty among the lowest-quartile families in 1991. These data indicate that upward mobility is significant for 1992–1993 college graduates relative to their economic backgrounds. Even so, correlations are also present between 1991 and 1997 economic class measures, suggesting that economic background is related to economic opportunities among college graduates.

Figure 5.7   Distribution of Economic Class, 1997 Households, 1992–1993 College Graduates

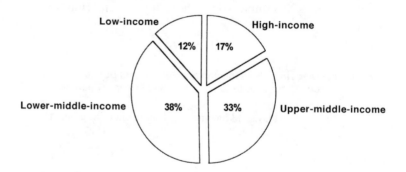

Source: National Center for Education Statistics (2000a).

Notes: Low: household income less than 1.85x poverty; Lower-middle: household income between 1.85–3.72x poverty; Upper-middle: household income between 3.72–6x poverty; High: household income greater than 6x poverty.

Tabular Comparison of Economic Class Position, 1991 and 1997

Table 5.2 shows that college graduates from low-income backgrounds are overrepresented among low-income households in 1997 and underrepresented among high-income households. Almost 39 percent of low-income households in 1997 were college graduates from low-income backgrounds, but less than 26 percent of 1997 households with incomes greater than six times poverty were from low-income family backgrounds. In contrast, only 15 percent of low-income households in 1997 consisted of college graduates from high-income backgrounds, and almost 22 percent of households with income greater than six times poverty in 1997 were from high-income backgrounds. These comparisons further suggest that the structural pattern of economic class inequality remains among college graduates alongside individual patterns of upward mobility.

Figure 5.8 illustrates that economic class in 1997 varies among households based on race and ethnicity. For example, 17 percent of white college graduates were among high-income households in 1997 compared to less than 10 percent of African American college graduates and 12 percent of Hispanic college graduates. In contrast, almost 16 percent of African American college graduates and 15 percent of Hispanic college graduates were

Table 5.2   Tabular Comparison of Economic Class Distributions in 1991 and 1997, 1992–1993 College Graduates (percentages)

	Low-Income 1991	Lower-Middle-Income 1991	Upper-Middle-Income 1991	High-Income 1991
Low-income 1997	38.6	22.9	23.5	15.0
Lower-middle income 1997	35.7	26.4	23.5	14.4
Upper-middle income 1997	30.4	24.5	28.5	16.6
High-income 1997	25.7	22.1	30.4	21.8
Overall 1991	32.6	24.6	26.3	16.4

Source: National Center for Education Statistics (2000a).
Notes: Gamma .125
P < .000

**Figure 5.8   Economic Class Distributions by Race and Ethnicity, 1997
Households, 1992–1993 College Graduates (percentages)**

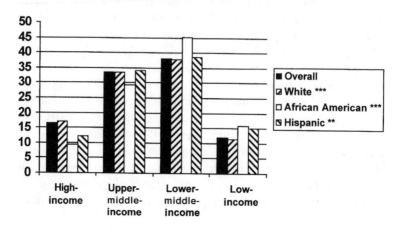

Source: National Center for Education Statistics (2000a).
Notes: *** P < .001, ** P < .01

among low-income households in 1997, whereas only 11 percent
of white college graduates were among low-income households in
1997.

Economic mobility patterns were significant for 1992–1993
college graduates across all race and ethnic groups; however, the
"correspondence principle" also holds true for African American
and white college graduates (see Figure 5.9). Among whites, 86
percent of college graduates from low-income backgrounds had
economic mobility by 1997. Almost half of white college graduates from lower-middle-income backgrounds had economic
mobility. At the same time, 53 percent of white high-income
households in 1997 consisted of college graduates from upper-
middle and high-income family backgrounds. Only 24 percent of
white high-income households consisted of college graduates
from low-income backgrounds. Thus, high-income white households were more than twice as likely to consist of students from
higher-income backgrounds (above the median poverty index in
1991) than low-income backgrounds.

A similar pattern exists for African American households: 83
percent of college graduates from low-income backgrounds had

economic mobility by 1997. More than one-third of African American college graduates from lower-middle-income backgrounds had economic mobility. Yet 55 percent of African American high-income households in 1997 consisted of college graduates from upper-middle and high-income backgrounds. Only 28 percent of African American high-income households consisted of college graduates from low-income backgrounds. Like white college graduates, high-income African American households in 1997 were about twice as likely to consist of students from family backgrounds above the median 1991 poverty index. Figure 5.9 illustrates this pattern of high-income households in 1997 for African American and white college graduates: a larger proportion of students from upper-middle and high-income backgrounds were in high-income households.

This pattern is not consistent among 1992–1993 Hispanic college graduates. For example, 81 percent of Hispanic college graduates from low-income families and 45 percent from lower-middle-income families had economic mobility by 1997.

Figure 5.9   **Percentages of High-Income Households in 1997 by Race and Ethnicity, Controlling for Economic Class Background, 1992–1993 College Graduates**

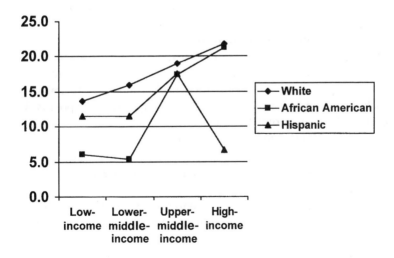

Source: National Center for Education Statistics (2000a).

However, 50 percent of high-income Hispanic households in 1997 consisted of college graduates from low-income family backgrounds. Only 28 percent of high-income Hispanic households consisted of college graduates from families with 1991 poverty index above the median. As Figure 5.9 shows, an almost equal proportion of high-income Hispanic households in 1997 were college graduates from families below and above the median 1991 poverty index. The structural pattern of economic class inequality does not remain among Hispanic college graduates in part because more than 75 percent were from lower-income family backgrounds.

Predicting the 1997 Poverty Index

A more sophisticated statistical test of the "correspondence principle" is multiple regression analysis on the 1997 poverty index, which provides estimates for the probability that household income among 1992–1993 college graduates is above the poverty threshold.[2] Using the *Baccalaureate and Beyond 1993/1997* longitudinal survey, measures of family background, race and ethnicity, marital status, undergraduate field of study, type of undergraduate institution, and educational attainment of the respondent were included in the statistical model along with total household educational debt. (See Appendix E, which provides the multiple regression results.)

The results indicate that marital status and receiving an undergraduate degree in engineering or the health professions are the strongest positive predictors of 1997 economic class position. However, economic class background and the type of undergraduate institution attended also strongly and positively predict 1997 economic class position. Moreover, racial background (African American) was a significant negative predictor of 1997 economic class position. Figure 5.10 illustrates the probabilities generated from the multiple regression estimates in the model.

Extrapolating from the estimates in the statistical model, African American college graduates had a poverty index .692 points lower than all college graduates in 1997. A lower poverty index means a lower economic class position. Hispanic married households also had a lower 1997 poverty index, but this finding

Figure 5.10 Odds Ratios, Exp (β), for Regression Estimates on 1997 Household Poverty Index, 1992–1993 College Graduates

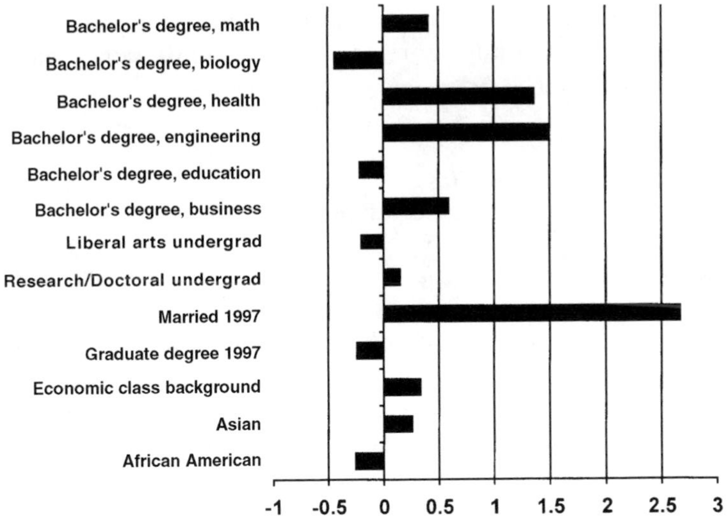

Source: National Center for Education Statistics (2000a).

was not significant among single Hispanic households. College graduates who were married or lived in a "marriage-like" relationship in 1997 had a poverty index almost 3 points higher than all college graduates. For example, a single student at the twenty-fifth percentile poverty index in 1997 (2.63) could more than double household income relative to the poverty threshold if he or she married (assuming that the spouse also worked, of course). Undergraduate field of study is also an important predictor of economic class position: engineering college graduates had a poverty index almost 2 points higher, and students with health profession degrees 2.2 points higher, than all college graduates in 1997.

Yet economic class background still matters despite these other statistical effects. Extrapolating from the multiple regression model: a college graduate from a high-income background had a poverty index 1.76 points higher in 1997 than a college graduate from a low economic class background. Put another way, for each

category increase in 1991 economic class position, the 1997
poverty index for college graduates increases .587 points. Thus, a
college graduate at the twenty-fifth percentile of the 1997 poverty
index (2.63) would have a poverty index 22 percent higher if he or
she had been from a lower-middle-income family rather than a
low-income family.

Conclusion: Economic Class Inequality Among College Graduates

The evidence from *Baccalaureate and Beyond 1993/1997* indicates that economic class background still influences the relative economic positions of college graduates. In other words,
students from low-income backgrounds who obtain a college
degree are more likely to have lower economic class positions
within the social system relative to other college graduates
from higher-income backgrounds. Thus, the "correspondence
principle" documented by Bowles and Gintis in the 1970s is
still operating, even among a select group of 1992–1993 college graduates. These patterns are also consistent with Collins's
credential society thesis. That is, even given higher education
credentials, structural inequality among groups remains empirically present. Thus, low-income students, African Americans,
and Hispanics remain in relatively disadvantageous locations
within the social system compared to upper-income and white
students.

Such evidence validates the theoretical premise of this
study: *obtaining a college education can provide individual
socioeconomic opportunities while simultaneously reinforcing
structural patterns of social inequality.* The overreliance on student loans to finance higher education is not the only reason for
this contradictory process. Even so, educational debt does place
an additional burden on students who already face significant
structural barriers to socioeconomic mobility. Moreover, students with excessive educational debt burden are more likely to
have lower economic class positions relative to other college
graduates four years after receiving a bachelor's degree.
Regardless of the level of educational debt burden, but especially among households with debt burden greater than 8 percent,

the everyday financial hardships are greatest for families in lower economic class positions.

Notes

1. These correlations are present between the theoretical economic class variable described above (.104) and between economic class quartiles (.114).

2. See Chapter 3 for details about *Baccalaureate and Beyond*.

6 Renewing the Promise: Innovative Policies to Improve Higher Education Opportunity

The discussion thus far has illustrated the premise of federal and state higher education policy: under federal policy, students borrow substantially to pay for higher education, while under state policy students and families are paying higher prices via tuitions and fees. Thus, the current federal and state political orientations favor the *individual* value of higher education rather than its *social* value. More precisely, the empirical evidence in Chapters 2–5 suggests that higher education policies are contributing to the reproduction of race, ethnic, and economic class inequality. Current public policies that help students and families finance higher education are incompatible with the transition to a global knowledge economy. Although globalization makes higher education increasingly important for individual socioeconomic opportunities, it also generates social, political, and cultural challenges. These challenges call for higher education to produce individuals willing and able to address the collective interests of an increasingly integrated global society.

In order for higher education to deliver on its promise of balancing instrumental self-interest and communicative social interest, current assumptions about higher education must be transformed. An innovative approach to higher education requires more integrative and complementary federal, state, and institutional policies. The purpose of this transformation is to make higher education more affordable for more students, regardless of their ability to pay—a goal that underpinned the original Higher Education Act of 1965. In short, the cornerstone of an integrated higher education policy must be to (1) reduce the share of college costs that families and students are expected to pay directly (i.e., via tuition and fees); and (2) reduce students' overreliance on loans to pay such costs.

Renewing the Promise of Higher Education

The philosophy of equal opportunities in higher education, as well as the social needs of an increasingly global society, point toward the expansion of universal public education to include education beyond high school. Ideally, this would mean a commitment from federal, state, and local governments and from business, civic, and philanthropic organizations to provide a postsecondary education at little or no cost to any student who is qualified for admission to public colleges and universities given the specific organization and mission of a state's higher education system (see sidebar: "Free Education for All"). More practically, tuition and fees at public colleges and universities must be sufficiently low so that upper-middle-income and high-income families can afford college without financial aid and so that federal and state grant financial aid can help low-income and lower-middle-income families pay for a college without requiring student loans. In most instances, direct costs (i.e., tuition and fees) as well as indirect costs (e.g., books, supplies, housing, food and beverages, and transportation) should *not* require borrowing at public colleges and universities.

In conjunction with setting low-tuition policies for public colleges and universities, federal and state higher education policy must entice private colleges and universities to use institutional resources to lower tuition and fees for students they admit based on students' and families' ability to pay. In practical terms, the formula that private colleges and universities use to determine financial need must be consistently applied to all students, and it also should include the state and federal grant funds available to each student only insofar as the private institution is committed to cover the gap between public grant aid and the tuition and fees charged. In this way, students from all economic circumstances would be assured that paying the direct costs for a private college and university would not require borrowing. If student loans are

Free Education for All

Adolph Reed Jr., a professor on the graduate faculty of Social and Political Science at the New School for Social Research, is a leading advocate for universal access to higher education (see generally Szymanski 2002; and Reed 2001). The model program of universal access is the GI Bill, officially known as the American Servicemen's Readjustment Act of 1944. The GI Bill paid for the postsecondary education of almost 8 million soldiers after World War II. Students received full tuition, fees, and family living stipends up to $1,440 (or $14,136 in 2001 dollars). A 1988 report of the congressional Subcommittee on Education and Health of the Joint Economic Committee stated that, by 1987, the GI Bill college attendees increased the nation's output of goods and services by $312 billion in current-year dollars. In addition, the report found that 40 percent of those who attended college on the GI Bill would not otherwise have done so. Overall, the report estimated that the GI Bill's investment in human capital returned $6.90 for every dollar spent (or more than $318 billion in 2001 dollars).

According to the National Center for Education Statistics (2003b), in 1999–2000 public colleges and universities received approximately $29 billion in revenue from student tuition and fees, including federally supported financial aid. Federal, state, and local governments provided an additional $79 billion. Thus, replacing tuition revenue from students and families with public resources would increase the social support of postsecondary education by 37 percent. If tuition replacement revenue was provided by the federal government, the additional $29 billion investment would account for about 3 percent of the $808 billion federal discretionary budget request for FY 2004 (see *Budget of the U.S. Government, Fiscal Year 2003*). Moreover, assuming the same social returns as estimated on the GI Bill, this $29 billion investment in human capital would return $200 billion to the national economy.

needed to pay indirect costs at private colleges and universities, or any other costs related to higher education, such borrowing should not result in excessive educational debt burden once students have graduated.

The integration of federal and state higher education policy presupposes three significant changes in existing federal financial aid programs. First, funding for federal Pell Grants should be increased and become an entitlement. Second, subsidized Stafford Loan limits should be increased so that lower-income students can attend more expensive colleges and universities, with the federal government paying the interest while the students are enrolled. Third, the federal student loan programs should cap the proportion of monthly income used to repay student debt for all students while maintaining a standard repayment period (e.g., ten years).

Federal and state policy integration also presupposes that state policymakers and higher education leaders reinvigorate their historical commitment to low tuitions at public colleges and universities. A federal-state partnership may require increased state investment in need-based grant programs so that the combined federal and state grant aid programs cover the total price of public postsecondary education for financially needy students.

Improving opportunities in higher education also calls for expanding access for lower-income students to private colleges and universities. Private institutions are important national and regional research and education centers and graduate many business, political, and civic leaders. A new federal-state partnership must encourage private colleges and universities to use institutional resources to supplement federal and state grant dollars for financially needy students. That is, private institutions need to increase grant aid so that tuition and fees do not require students to use educational loans.

These proposed changes in federal, state, and institutional higher education policies represent necessary steps to expand access to postsecondary education, as well as to ensure that college graduates are not constrained to make choices regarding continuing education and their careers based upon their ability to pay back student loans—a situation that favors instrumental self-interest over communicative social interest and thereby the reproduction of social inequality.

Federal Higher Education Policy

First and foremost, it is imperative that federal financial aid policy authorizes the Pell Grant as an entitlement. Unlike student loans, which are an entitlement to all students who qualify, the Pell Grant must be appropriated annually during the budgetary process. Subsequently, the annual Pell Grant appropriation is calculated based on the estimated number of eligible students and the authorized maximum Pell Grant ($4,050 in fiscal year 2002–2003). If the appropriation level of the Pell Grant program is insufficient, all students do not receive the maximum Pell Grant to which they are eligible without additional legislative budget appropriations. According to the College Board (2002b), the Pell Grant program received almost $10 billion in 2001–2002. Yet this appropriation was underfunded by at least $1 billion because of higher financial need and larger numbers of students in the Pell eligibility pool.

If the Pell Grant program were to become an entitlement to all eligible students, then the federal grant amount that a student from any eligible family background would receive could be widely known and communicated with certainty. For example, any student with an expected family contribution of zero could be guaranteed the maximum Pell Grant. In fact, if federal methodology were to target an "automatic zero" expected family contribution to all students who qualify for the Free and Reduced Lunch program in secondary school, the assurance of federal financial aid could be made to students in middle school. Currently, such a guarantee cannot be made because annual budget appropriations occur much later than the period during which high school students make decisions about whether, and where, to attend college. Moreover, colleges and universities that admit Pell-eligible students do not know in advance the eventual Pell Grant amount for such students. This problem repeats itself annually.

Current federal policy regulating the Pell Grant does not adequately serve the needs of students from low economic class backgrounds in two ways. First, although low-income students may not know how much federal grant money they will receive, they can know the amount of loans for which they are eligible. At best, these students do not know which colleges are affordable with and without loans. At worst, they may erroneously believe that loans are the only type of financial aid available. This lack of information is a critical barrier to higher education opportunities because students and parents consistently overestimate the price of college.

According to the American Council on Education (2002b), the average adult believes tuition and fees at public four-year colleges is more than $11,500, which is three times higher than the national average. Similarly, the National Center for Education Statistics (2001a) reports that two-thirds of sixth-grade through twelfth-grade students with postsecondary education aspirations, and 46 percent of their parents, could not estimate tuition and fees for the college they planned to attend. Of those who could estimate tuition and fees, 38 percent of parents with incomes above $75,000 made accurate estimates, compared to only 12 percent of parents with incomes below $15,000, 19 percent of parents with incomes between $15,000 and $30,000, and 25 percent of parents with incomes between $30,000 and $50,000. Thus, a significant majority of students and parents are uninformed about the cost of college.

Second, colleges and universities that serve low-income students must estimate financial aid packages that may not bear out if the Pell Grant appropriation is insufficient. Thus, each year postsecondary institutions may have to adjust the grant amounts for low-income students after they enroll once the final Pell Grant amounts are determined. These post-hoc decisions by financial aid administrators can increase the need for low-income students to rely on loans to pay for college. This situation is especially problematic for colleges with limited resources that serve large numbers of Pell-eligible students; these postsecondary institutions cannot readily make up any federal grant shortfall with institutional grant dollars. Given such circumstances, students from low economic class backgrounds are at a disadvantage in the process because the Pell Grant is not an entitlement.

It is also important for federal higher education policy to increase the availability of subsidized student loans and decrease the need for unsubsidized loans among Pell Grant–eligible students. The 1992 reauthorization of the Higher Education Act increased the maximum cumulative amount that undergraduate students could borrow to $23,000. At the same time, without increasing the maximum subsidized Stafford Loan for first- and second-year students, the 1992 reauthorization created an unsubsidized guaranteed student loan that was not need-based. Any student can qualify for an unsubsidized federal loan, but the federal government does not pay the interest on those loans for students while they are enrolled. Thus, subsidized federal loans are preferable for student borrowers because the government pays the interest on the loan while the student is enrolled at least half-time in a qualified postsecondary institution.

One reason that overall loan use increased substantially after 1992 is that the annual dollar volume of unsubsidized Stafford Loans increased from zero to $8.7 billion between 1992–1993 and 1995–1996 and almost doubled again between 1995–1996 and 2001–2002 to $17 billion (College Board 2002b). Thus, cumulative student borrowing of unsubsidized student loans exceeded $99 billion between 1992 and 2002. In constant dollars, total annual borrowing between 1995–1996 and 2001–2002 increased 30 percent; however, the dollar volume of unsubsidized loans increased by 69 percent while subsidized loans increased by only 3 percent. In 2001–2002, students borrowed more than $41 billion in federal loans, of which 41 percent was unsubsidized.

The maximum subsidized Stafford Loan for first-year students ($2,625) has not changed since 1986, yet the total price for college increased more than 30 percent in real dollars during the same period. The result is more students using more and larger unsubsidized educational loans to help pay for college. According to the National Center for Education Statistics, 21 percent of dependent students from the lowest family income quartiles who borrowed for college in 1999–2000, and 60 percent of independent low-income students who borrowed, received unsubsidized Stafford Loans. A much larger proportion of dependent student borrowers from the highest family income quartile (74 percent) received unsubsidized Stafford Loans in 1999–2000 (National Center for Education Statistics 2003a).

Although many borrowers of unsubsidized loans do not qualify for need-based financial aid, students from lower economic class backgrounds use unsubsidized loans because the federal Pell Grant and subsidized loan maximums are insufficient to cover the total price of college. The government guarantee against student loan default makes both subsidized and unsubsidized student loans equally profitable to lenders. However, by encouraging borrowers with unsubsidized loans to capitalize their interest while students are enrolled rather than pay the interest, the cost to the student as well as the profit to the lender can be increased considerably. Furthermore, the increased use of unsubsidized loans for low-income students, and the additional cost of these loans resulting from capitalized interest, can lead to more financial hardship and increased educational debt burden after graduation.

As long as federal guaranteed loans remain a considerable portion of student financial aid, the amount of loans students with demonstrable financial need can borrow via the subsidized loan program should be increased, albeit without increasing the cumulative maximum loan amount. For students who continue to use unsubsidized Stafford Loans, federal policy should enforce regulations that require full disclosure of the increased cost of the loan and written consent from the borrower before lenders can capitalize the interest on those loans. Furthermore, if interest is capitalized on unsubsidized student loans, the additional interest charges should be deducted from any default costs the government pays on those loans. Because most private colleges and universities do not receive state appropriations, and thus have higher tuition and fees than most public colleges and universities, an important byproduct of increasing the borrowing limits of subsidized Stafford Loans is to make private colleges a reasonable option for students from low economic class backgrounds. If college choices are expanded for low-income students, then opportunities in higher education can be improved.

Finally, federal higher education policy must address the increasing educational debt burden that many college graduates face, especially those from low-income, African American, and Hispanic backgrounds. One way to counter this growing problem is to cap educational debt repayment as a proportion of gross annual income and limit the loan repayment period. Over the past decade average cumulative undergraduate debt has almost doubled to $18,000. Adults with graduate degrees have even higher total educational debt: in 1997, average educational debt for students with graduate degrees was more than $27,000, but it can exceed $100,000 for students training to become doctors and lawyers. Regardless of the amount that a student borrows to help pay for higher education, the terms of debt repayment should be based on annual student earnings after graduation for a standard period of time (e.g., ten years).[1]

The U.S. Department of Education and the student loan industry recommend the maximum monthly educational debt burden to be 8 percent of gross monthly income. Since 1993, student borrowers with multiple educational loans can consolidate at lower interest rates, but the new lower monthly debt must be repaid over fifteen, twenty, or even thirty years. Mortgaging a postsecondary education for thirty years is not a reasonable solution to excessive educational debt burden.[2] Rather, education debt repayment policy should be progressive—students should pay a statutory portion of gross monthly income for a standard repayment period. In England, college students use loans to cover basic living expenses while enrolled. Those loans are then repaid at a zero-percent real interest rate for twelve years based on the student's earnings; in this way, educational debt is equitably distributed across society.

If educational debt repayment were a fixed proportion of gross monthly income, then college graduates would be more able to make career and occupational choices based on personal and societal interests rather than financial imperatives. Consequently, college graduates could pursue work opportunities in employment sectors that improve the collective well-being of society, including education, social welfare, and community service as well as the nonprofit sector in general, which typically pays lower wages compared to for-profit enterprises. An additional desirable outcome could be an increase in the numbers of artists, musicians, poets, and writers who can pursue their dreams and benefit society without the financial weight of student loans redirecting their talents. In short, if student loans are necessary to finance higher education for growing numbers of citizens, then the resulting debt burden associated with these loans should not be excessive. Simply put, the occupational choices of college graduates should not be primarily influenced by the financial imperative to repay educational loans.

A second way to address the educational debt burden is to expand loan forgiveness programs. The widespread existence of such programs at the federal and state levels indicates that policymakers already understand that the reliance on student loans to finance higher education has unintended consequences: loans can result in significant debt burden for students once they enter the repayment period, and that debt can be a disincentive for recruiting college graduates to career fields that address the collective needs of society such as teaching. During the current reauthorization of the Higher Education Act, the Alliance for Equity in Higher Education (2003) proposed a federal loan forgiveness entitlement targeted at areas of national need, such as advanced scientific fields, race and ethnic minority health, teacher education, and social services.

State Higher Education Policy

Because state appropriations represent the largest single revenue stream for most public colleges and universities, states have considerable leverage over the tuition and fees charged to students. In conjunction with the federal policy reforms discussed above, direct state appropriations to public higher education should be linked to targeted tuition and fee levels that take into account the economic circumstances of each state. Moreover, targeted tuition levels should limit erratic swings in tuition that raise the price of college beyond the grasp of students from disadvantageous positions within the social system. One way for states to peg tuition at public four-year institutions is to target a reasonable level based on students' and families' ability to pay. For example, tuition and fees could be tied to a general economic index, such as state gross domestic product per capita (Hauptman 2001). If states were to set tuition and fee levels based on economic conditions and students' and families' ability to pay, the public sector's direct costs would vary with state economic growth.

Alternatively, tuition and fees could be tied to a particular ratio of the total cost of college that students and families are expected to pay. Currently, the portion of general and educational expenditures paid for by tuition and fees is 36 percent. That figure is higher than the recommended share that students and families should pay (30 percent) based on a widely heralded 1973 report from the Carnegie Commission on Higher Education. Given the significant income inequalities we see today, the higher price of attending college, as well as the need for more students to receive a postsecondary education for individual and societal benefits, a more reasonable portion would be 25 percent.

Financial Aid Policy at Colleges and Universities

Along with additional targeted federal and state resources for higher education, public and private colleges and universities need to increase their commitment to need-based financial aid in order to expand the choices for all students who seek a college education. Although colleges and universities bear significant responsibility for the low or high cohort graduation rates of college students, financial aid policy is an important factor that contributes to the lack of widespread student success. In 1999–2000, about one-fourth of undergraduates at private not-for-profit four-year institutions and more than one-third of undergraduates at public four-year colleges and universities who received the maximum subsidized Stafford Loan had at least two risk characteristics associated with not persisting or attaining a bachelor's degree (National Center for Education Statistics 2003a). These borrowers are most likely to be from low-income backgrounds.

Because the overreliance on student loans to pay for college is related to lower student persistence and attainment, increased grant aid may be a fundamental component for improved student outcomes. Michael McPherson and Morton Schapiro (1998) suggest that the goal of federal financial aid policy should be to ensure that need-based aid does not erode and thus undermine the opportunity for students from lower-income backgrounds to obtain a college degree. They conclude that the key federal policy lever is to use increased funding for the Pell Grant as an incentive for colleges and universities to increase grant financial aid to needy students.

Let's use the Pell Grant entitlement described above as an example: the Pell Grant could flow through colleges and universities only if they were willing to match the federal grant for eligible students who enroll in their institutions. Because colleges and universities face significantly different financial circumstances, the source of this "institutional match" could be state financial aid sources, private scholarship sources, institutional endowment sources, or some combination thereof. The intended outcome for leveraging institutional grant aid through a Pell Grant entitlement would be to reduce the need for student loans to finance higher education and thus expand opportunities for students from all economic circumstances (but especially lower-income students) to attend public as well as private colleges and universities.

Strategies to influence institutional behavior are not limited to the federal government. In fact, a more significant lever exists between state policy and institutional behavior. State direct appropriations represent the single largest revenue stream for public colleges and universities, and, in some states, grant programs are available to students who enroll in public as well as private colleges. Because public postsecondary institutions enroll the majority of students from low-income, African American, and Hispanic families, state allocations are perhaps the most powerful lever state policymakers possess to encourage postsecondary institutions to change. For example, states could create allocation formulas for direct appropriations that reward public and private colleges for serving students from disadvantaged backgrounds (Hauptman 2001).

Demographic trends indicate that low-income students, first-generation students, and students from African American and Hispanic families represent the largest share of the growth in the future college applicant pool. According to the Advisory Committee on Student Financial Assistance (2001), 80 percent of the growth in the traditional college-age population from 2001 to 2015 will be from those with Hispanic, Asian, black, and Native American backgrounds. Students from such backgrounds are typically less prepared for college academically, financially, and culturally, and thus their education is more costly for colleges and universities.

One way to increase the persistence and attainment rate of college students, without reducing access for those from disadvantaged backgrounds, is for state higher education budgets to provide supplemental appropriations for public *and* private colleges that enroll students from lower economic class backgrounds. In other words, public colleges and universities could receive a per-student appropriation based on enrollments and an additional appropriation for enrollments of Pell-eligible students. The additional appropriation could be used for academic and social support services intended to improve the success rate of all students. An additional appropriation for enrolling Pell-eligible students could also be extended to private colleges and universities in the state. In this way, targeted state appropriations would provide additional resources for colleges and universities that enroll Pell-eligible students, which could be used for academic and support services and thus expand the opportunity for students from low-income backgrounds to succeed in college.

A public policy commitment of this magnitude cannot occur without institutional accountability for successfully educating students to pursue individual self-interest and to contribute to the social good. Over the past several years, concerns over accountability in higher education among state policymakers have led to the increased use of performance-based funding formulas for public colleges and universities (Zumeta 2001). In 1997, thirty-seven states reported using performance measures in higher educational policymaking, and twenty-three reported using them in the budgetary process; these measures often link additional state support to specific student outcomes, such as student persistence and attainment (Zumeta 2001).

Although such tactics by state policymakers are widespread, the actual measures used to determine accountability remain crude and are often inconsistent with the full-range of desired outcomes expected from public colleges and universities. That is to say, there is little evidence that the current practice of performance-based funding, in and of itself, helps rebalance the individual and social purposes of higher education. Even so, the political interest in accountability could dovetail with the need for more integrated policies across federal, state, and institutional levels.

The accountability measures for public and private colleges and universities could be set at reasonable benchmarks based on the predicted success rates of the students that colleges admit.[3] That is, a supplemental state appropriation for enrolling low-income students could be linked to important accountability goals like degree attainment. If any public college were unable to meet the benchmarks, it would lose eligibility for the supplemental appropriation.[4] If any private college were unable to meet benchmarks of student success, it would no longer qualify for the supplemental appropriation or be eligible to participate in state need-based and non–need-based grant programs.

An Integrated Vision for Higher Education Policy

The need for a more integrated higher education policy across federal, state, and institutional levels is widely known among higher education policy analysts, financial aid administrators, many college and university presidents, as well as some individuals within higher education associations, policymaking bodies, businesses, community organizations, and foundations. A central outcome of an integrated higher education policy should be more affordable public and private colleges and universities. A necessary first step in making higher education more affordable is to restore the historic balance between grants and loans in federal and state financial aid policy. In most states, access to public higher education without borrowing is limited to two-year colleges for low-income dependent students; there is virtually no loan-free access to public colleges and universities for low-income adult students (Kipp, Price, and Wohlford 2002). Thus, one fundamental objective of integrating policies would be to reduce the overreliance on student loans, thereby making public higher education affordable without the need to borrow.

Although the federal government provides only 15 percent of the total support for higher education, it provides more than two-thirds of student financial aid. In 2001–2002, total federal spending through the Pell Grant and Supplemental Education Opportunity Grant was twice as much as all state grant financial aid combined ($10.6 billion versus $5 billion). Moreover, in 1999 ten states provided almost three-fourths of the total need-based grant aid ($2.8 billion of $3.8 billion); in twenty-three other states the combined total need-based grant aid was less than $100 million (National Association of State Student Grant and Aid Programs 2003).

One way to link federal and state higher education policy could be to use a new and larger Pell Grant entitlement to entice states to peg tuition and fees at public four-year colleges and universities to a level at or below the federal Pell Grant maximum or, alternatively, at some level related to students' and families' ability to pay. States would most likely use one of the following two policy tools to ensure that students in their state qualify for the higher Pell Grant: (1) provide additional need-based grant aid to fill the gap between the higher Pell Grant and tuition and fee levels; or (2) increase direct appropriations in order to lower tuition and fees to a prescribed level. In states that already have low tuition and fees, the larger Pell Grant could be used to pay indirect college costs.

A second way to leverage federal grant financial aid is to link more funding for those programs with expanded second-tier state grant programs. For example, Title IV of the Higher Education Act authorizes federal matching funds via the Leveraging Educational Assistance Program (LEAP) for state need-based grants. In 2001–2002, about $50 million was appropriated for this program, which leveraged an additional $100 million in state grant financial aid (College Board 2002b). Ed St. John, a professor of higher education at Indiana University, affixes the policy solution to improved college access and affordability at the state level.[5] Rather than prescribe a level of tuition and fees that states must target in order for residents to receive a higher Pell Grant, he argues, federal matching dollars should be increased to encourage states to provide additional grant aid for financially needy students. Based on the current LEAP formula, for every new dollar in state need-based grant aid, the federal government would add 50 cents. In this way, students from low economic class backgrounds can receive more grants and fewer loans to help pay for college. Moreover, because the additional grant aid is from a federal-state partnership, the pressure to raise tuitions in order to increase financial aid for low-income students is reduced—an important outcome given the current political demands from the voting electorate (St. John 2003, esp. chap. 9).

The Need for a Statutory Financial Aid Formula: Modeling a New STEP

In 1993, the National Commission on Responsibilities for Financing Postsecondary Education released a report, *Making College Affordable Again*, in which it articulated a concept called the Student Total Education Package (STEP). The purpose of STEP was to ensure that any full-time undergraduate student would receive a set amount of federal financial aid. But the type of aid would vary according to the student's financial need and the price of attendance (financial aid for part-time attendance would be prorated). In 1992, the total amount of federal aid available to an individual under STEP would have been $14,000 based on a weighted national average of per-student expenditures at four-year institutions. Depending on the student's economic circumstances, the $14,000 would consist of some combination of grants, work-study, and subsidized student loans. The maximum grant was $4,000. The intent of STEP was to provide predictable sources and levels of federal financial aid that all students could depend on to help pay for college.

Since 1992, the total price that colleges charge students and families has increased 28 percent and 30 percent at public and private four-year institutions, respectively (College Board 2002a). Adjusting the STEP estimate accordingly, a reasonable increase given the current budgetary environment for states, would yield a revised target of $18,000. Based on the 1993 STEP formula, the total federal financial aid package would consist of roughly 30 percent grants and 70 percent loans. This imbalance between grants and loans is not conducive to improving higher education opportunities, especially because low-income students are at increased risk of excessive educational debt burden after graduation from college (see Chapter 4).

In 2001–2002, the average for tuition and fees at public four-year colleges was $3,725 and the average total price $9,000 (College Board 2002a). In order for public higher education to be affordable without borrowing, approximately $9,000 in grant financial aid is needed to help students with the most financial need. In 2002–2003, the maximum Pell Grant was authorized at $4,050. Increasing the Pell Grant maximum to $7,500, and then leveraging this increase with states to gain an additional $1,500 in grant financial aid (or lower tuition and fees), means that the average total cost of attendance at public four-year colleges would be affordable through grant financial aid. Under this model, a more equitable ratio of federal grants to loans would be at least 40 percent grants ($7,500) and no more than 60 percent work-study and loans ($10,500) depending on the price of the college. More important, the federal loan portion should be subsidized for lower-income and middle-income families who will need additional financial aid to attend more expensive colleges and universities.

At the same time, the $3,500 increase in the federal Pell Grant maximum can be used to leverage private colleges and universities to admit Pell-eligible students and match the grant with "institutional grant dollars." For private colleges with large endowments, increasing grant aid for low-income students by $3,500 is not difficult. In fact, Princeton University has a need-blind admission policy and guarantees that no student admitted will receive loans in their financial aid package. Many other private and public colleges that serve larger numbers of low-income students will find it difficult to match the increased Pell Grant with institutional resources. In these instances, the state grant aid match of $1,500 and a state supplemental appropriation for enrolling a low-income student could be counted as part of this so-called institutional match.

If we use as a benchmark the net price of college after federal grants in 1999–2000 provided by the National Center for Education Statistics (2002c), increasing the Pell Grant to $7,500 and leveraging an additional state and institutional match of $3,500 would reduce the net price (after federal grants) at private research and doctoral institutions for students from the lowest income quartile by 30 percent to $17,100. Making the same assumptions, the net price (after federal grants) at private comprehensive and baccalaureate colleges and universities for students from the lowest income quartile would fall by 47 percent to $7,950. Because the state and institutional match are new dollars, and assuming current state and institutional grants remained unchanged, the estimated total federal, state, and institutional grant aid for students from the lowest income quartile at private research and doctoral universities would be approximately $19,500; at private comprehensive and baccalaureate institutions it would be roughly $14,500. Thus, total federal, state, and institutional grant aid would cover the direct costs (i.e., tuition and fees) at private colleges and universities.

To recap: increasing the federal Pell Grant maximum to $7,500 represents the grant portion of a new $18,000 Student Total Education Package of available federal financial aid. The new Pell Grant, combined with a $1,500 state match via lower tuition and fees or increased state grant financial aid, makes public higher education affordable to all students without the need to borrow. In addition, by leveraging the additional Pell Grant dollars to encourage private colleges and universities to increase grant aid for low-income students by $3,500 (from institutional, state, and private sources), combined grant aid based on 1999–2000 net-price calculations at private colleges and universities for low-income students would cover roughly 77 percent of the total cost of attendance at comprehensive and baccalaureate institutions and 69 percent of the total cost at research and doctoral institutions. The remaining financial need for students from the lowest income backgrounds can be met by federal student loans and work-study (estimated at $10,500 for a revised STEP). These loans should be subsidized for low-income students so that interest will not accrue to students while they are enrolled.

Revisiting "Maintenance of Effort"

Prior to the 1986 amendments to the Higher Education Act, colleges participating in campus-based federal financial aid programs (i.e., work-study and Supplemental Educational Opportunity Grants) were required to maintain their institutional commitment to financial aid from year to year. In other words, federal policymakers wanted to ensure that colleges and universities did not replace their own financial aid with new federal dollars, which would have undermined the effectiveness of the campus-based federal programs. This provision was repealed for campus-based aid programs in 1986.

Maintenance of effort is still required for states in the federal LEAP program. LEAP provides matching federal dollars to states that commit new resources to their own need-based financial aid programs. By reconceptualizing the definition of "maintenance of effort" to include all Title IV financial aid programs, federal policy could effectively implement a STEP program without the risk of states or colleges reallocating their own dollars to capture new federal monies. For instance, "maintenance of effort" could be defined as the combined federal, state, and institutional grant aid pegged to a specific percentage of the total price of college for Pell-eligible students. In this way, any necessary reallocation of state or institutional resources, or any increases in college costs, would not harm financially needy students. In other words, states and institutions would risk the loss of new federal financial aid resources if they implemented policies that increased tuitions (and the total price) for low-income students.

Several implications for federal, state, and institutional policies are plausible byproducts of leveraging maintenance of effort in the way described above. First, because the additional federal grant dollars are targeted to financially needy students through an expanded Pell Grant entitlement, the financial incentive for colleges and universities will be to recruit and admit Pell-eligible students. Second, because the revised STEP model described above requires a state match and is pegged to tuition based on students' and families' ability to pay, the incentive for state policymakers will be to maintain low-tuition levels or increase financial aid when tuitions rise. Thus, "maintenance of effort" could encourage cost containment by states and colleges. Finally, "maintenance of effort" represents a legislative mechanism to encourage complementary federal, state, and institutional policies that increase access for more students, especially low-income students, African Americans, and Hispanics.

Remodeling the Federal Guaranteed Student Loan Program

Given this outline of a new STEP, it seems apparent that federal student loans are necessary for students to attend more expensive (essentially private) colleges and universities. However, the use of student loans to finance higher education should not result in excessive educational debt burden for college graduates during repayment. Moreover, subsidized loans are preferable for student borrowers because the government pays the interest while the student is enrolled. Under the new STEP model described above, the maximum federal loan would be $18,000 for students who do not qualify for the federal Pell Grant or college work-study but who still exhibit financial need. A student who qualifies for the new maximum Pell Grant of $7,500 under this model would be eligible for $10,500 in federal student loans.

The current guaranteed student loan program consists of the Federal Family Education Loan Program (FFELP), which relies on private capital markets, and the Direct Student Loan Program that was created by the 1992 reauthorization of the Higher Education Act and bypasses the private capital market. In 2001–2002, direct student lending provided about $11 billion in financial aid, and FFELP provided almost $30 billion in financial aid. Both of these programs offer subsidized loans to students with demonstrable need as measured by federal need analysis in addition to unsubsidized loans to students regardless of financial need. Under the new STEP program, the portion of the federal student loan that is subsidized should be based on the demonstrable financial need of the student, but it should not exceed the maximum value of federal student aid based on STEP (i.e., $18,000). In no instance should students receive federal grants or loans that exceed the total cost of attendance at public or private colleges and universities.

During the 1990s, several higher education leaders and federal policymakers proposed replacing the current student loan program with a federal student loan bank (Mumper 1996). For example, Robert Reischauer, former director of the Congressional Budget Office, proposed a "social insurance" model for federal student loans. Under this model, students would borrow money from a federal education trust and repay their debt through the existing social security payroll tax system. Reischauer estimated that student borrowers would pay 1 to 3 percent payroll tax on earned income for their lifetime (Reischauer 1993). These repayments would then provide capital for future student borrowers.

One problem with this approach is that it completely removes private capital markets from the federal student loan program. That outcome is not likely, politically speaking, given the economic power of an industry that lent students more than $350 billion between 1991–1992 and 2001–2002. Moreover, the Student Loan Marketing Association (known commonly as Sallie Mae, now operating as USA Education Inc.), was actually created as a government-sponsored enterprise by the Education Amendments of 1972.[6] A second problem with the social insurance model is the notion that student borrowers should have to repay throughout their working lifetimes. It seems more reasonable to model student loan repayments on the progressive income tax, which expects people with higher incomes to pay more in taxes than people with lower incomes.

The Ford Direct Student Loan Program may be the appropriate vehicle for implementing an education trust (e.g., education insurance entitlement), because 25 percent of federal guaranteed loans are already borrowed through that program. Therefore, one source of income for an education trust could be repayments from borrowers in the Direct Loan Program. Under this trust concept, the federal government originates loans to students, thereby saving the taxpayer-subsidized interest costs. More important, an education trust should also establish progressive debt repayment principles that limit monthly debt payments to 8 to 10 percent of monthly income for ten years. In this way, education loan repayments would be set according to gross monthly income rather than cumulative educational debt. Although some students with high educational debt and low earnings would end up repaying less than under the current loan program, many others with higher earnings (and thus the ability to make larger monthly payments) would repay more than under the current program.

Revenue for an education trust could also be raised by taxing capitalized interest payments received by lenders from unsubsidized student loans in the Federal Family Education Loan Program. That is, lenders who receive capitalized interest payments would be required to share that income with the education trust. A third possible revenue stream for an education trust could be an annual fee paid by the private capital market based on the current portfolio value of subsidized student loans in deferment (these loans currently earn interest paid by the federal government). These three sources could provide capital for future student loans funded through an education trust. If the profitability of student loans were reduced, it can be argued, many lenders would opt out of the student loan market, leaving only the most economically efficient businesses. Given that federal student loans are guaranteed against default—meaning guaranteed returns and virtually no risk to lenders—such an outcome is unlikely.

A more substantive and economically efficient reform for creating an education trust would be to make the Ford Direct Student Loan Program the capital market for all new education loans. To generate capital for new education loans, the current portfolio of subsidized loans in the direct lending program that are in repayment could be sold as an asset to the secondary loan market. The revenue from that sale would form an education trust to generate loans for new borrowers. The education trust could also generate revenue from unsubsidized loan interest payments, which under the new STEP would be paid only by higher-income borrowers. In addition, the savings represented by the cessation of interest payments on subsidized loans to private lenders could be a fourth source of revenue for the education trust. Under this plan, the education trust would hold all student loans as an asset as long as the borrower was enrolled in college. After graduation, the student loans would be bundled and sold to the secondary loan market. Banks in that private capital market would collect the monthly loan payments based on a statutory maximum educational debt burden of 8 to 10 percent.

Under this model of reform, profits in the private secondary market would be based on the future earnings of college graduates, rather than the actual value of the student loan portfolio. In other words, the future cumulative earnings of borrowers would determine the market value of a given portfolio of student loans. Because earnings are correlated to educational attainment, college major, and family background variables, the economic interests of the private secondary student loan market could lead to the selection of loans with the highest potential returns. Thus, the education trust would need to bundle loans to include a mix of borrowers with different earning trajectories.

There could be an interesting side-effect of this type of guaranteed student loan program. Secondary student loan market providers would recognize that ongoing wage differentials between students from different race and ethnic backgrounds, and low salaries in fields with high social value such as education and social services, are not in their economic self-interest. Imagine if the financial sector of the U.S. economy took a more public and proactive stance to raise salaries among teachers, social workers, and others who were employed in community-based organizations. In other words, an education trust organized within the federal government as the loan originator, which then sells bundles of guaranteed student loans to the private sector once the loans enter repayment, creates a socially valuable profit incentive. The secondary student loan market could increase profitability by encouraging businesses, corporations, nonprofit organizations, and federal, state, and local governments to pay higher wages.

Conclusion: Designing Public Policy to Increase the Social Value of Higher Education

This book has provided evidence to describe how current policy limits the opportunities of disadvantaged persons to pursue higher education. For low-income students, African Americans, and Hispanics who overcome the barriers to higher education and obtain a college degree, educational debt burden can be excessive.

During the past decade, federal financial aid policy did not generate a Pell Grant that kept pace with rising college prices. As a result, students increasingly relied on unsubsidized student loans to pay for college. At the same time, state increases in direct appropriations were inadequate to cover the costs associated with increased college enrollments, which resulted in higher tuitions. Finally, colleges and universities have shifted institutional financial aid resources to higher-income students (Davis 2003). And they have not provided sufficient academic and social support services for low-income students. Thus, students and families are paying a larger share of the total cost of higher education, a share that is paid increasingly with student loans. The consequence of these current higher education policies is the reproduction of race, ethnic, gender, and economic class inequality.

Put differently, higher education benefits individuals as well as society. Yet the overreliance on student loans undermines the social value of higher education by constraining the choices of students after they graduate. That is, students must follow the financial imperative of pursuing high-paying occupations that allow them to repay their college debt lest they face financial penalties (e.g., an excessive debt burden that they can't meet or a mortgage-like repayment term of, say, twenty or thirty years). The overreliance on student loans also contributes to unequal individual returns on higher education. In the first place, borrowers, based on a standard student loan repayment period of ten years, pay 33 percent more for the portion of college they financed with education loans than do nonborrowers. In addition, educational debt burden reduces the return on the higher education investment of borrowers during their early careers. Furthermore, low-income and African American college graduates are at much greater risk of having a debt burden that exceeds the 8 percent threshold. In the simplest terms, loans *increase* the price of college, whereas grants *reduce* the price.

In sum, current federal financial aid policy is regressive: it places a burden on students from disadvantaged backgrounds, especially low-income students and African Americans, that high-income students and affluent white students generally do not face. The regressive nature of federal financial aid policy stems primarily from its overreliance on student loans. A more innovative higher education policy that improves college opportunities and reinvigorates the social value of higher education requires changes in federal, state, and institutional policies.

Five pillars of public policy reform are listed below. Although no single idea presented here is necessarily the panacea, several key components are necessary for an integrated higher education policy to expand opportunities in higher education for all students regardless of economic or cultural backgrounds.

• First, the Pell Grant must be increased and made an entitlement so that the level of funding for that program can be reliable and widely communicated.

• Second, tuition and fees at public colleges and universities must be pegged more effectively to students' and families' ability to pay.

• Third, the use of loans by students with demonstrable need must primarily be subsidized; if unsubsidized loans are still needed, lenders should not be able to capitalize interest without full disclosure of the additional costs to the borrower.

• Fourth, the occupational choices of college graduates should not be predetermined by educational debt or come with financial hardships like an excessive debt burden. Thus, loan repayments should be capped so as to not exceed 8 to 10 percent of gross monthly income while maintaining a standard loan repayment period.

• Fifth, in exchange for a renewed public commitment to equal opportunities in higher education, colleges and universities must be held accountable for the success rates of students they admit.

These five pillars of reform in higher education policy should be integrated across federal, state, and institutional levels. The suggestions provided in this chapter are intended to provoke a more thoughtful discussion among the invested parties of the higher education community, including educators, social activists, policymakers, researchers and scholars, business and civic leaders, and current and future college students and their families. The motivation behind these ideas is to improve opportunities in higher education for all, as well as to expand options for students from disadvantaged backgrounds. The promise of higher education is that it provides socioeconomic opportunities for individuals as well as collective benefits for society. As the twenty-first century unfolds and globalization strengthens the interconnectedness of the world's people, it is imperative that higher education produce an educated citizenry ready and able to work collectively to improve the well-being of all members of society, not simply the most privileged.

Notes

1. See www.myrichuncle.com. In 2001, a group of investors led by Vishal Garg and Raza Khan launched a privately funded company that provides money to students for college in return for a fixed proportion of their monthly income for the ten years following the receipt of a bachelor's degree (fifteen years following a graduate degree). In the example on the website, a student pays 2.5 percent of his or her gross future income for ten years, beginning six months after graduation. However, the percentage of future income required varies among students in this program, based on their expected future earnings and on the price of the college(s) attended.

2. Less than 1 percent of new borrowers at schools that offer direct federal loans choose income-contingent repayment. The results of a survey of law school graduates suggests that the twenty-five-year repayment schedule is a disincentive to many prospective users of an income-contingent repayment program because it significantly increases the total amount to be repaid and because "loan forgiveness seems on the other side of a lifetime." See P. G. Schrag (2002), *Repay As You Earn: The Flawed Government Program to Help Students Have Public Service Careers* (Westport, CT: Bergin and Garvey).

3. The Lumina Foundation for Education is developing an index to measure the value-added impact of colleges, controlling for the characteristics of students they admit.

4. Community colleges represent a special kind of public institution. Not only do community colleges enroll significant numbers of low-income students; they also enroll students with divergent success goals. Accountability measures for community colleges cannot be solely based on degree attainment measures. Additional measures of student success are course completion

rates, occupational certificate attainment, and transfer rates to four-year institutions.

5. E. P. St. John (2003), *Refinancing the College Dream: Access, Equal Opportunity, and Justice for Taxpayers* (Baltimore: Johns Hopkins University Press).

6. In 2008, Sallie Mae will become completely independent of the federal government.

Appendices

Appendix A   Family Income Ranges Corresponding with Economic Class Variable, 1991

Economic Class	Family Size = 2	Family Size = 3
Upper-income (> 6X poverty)	Greater than $54,936	Greater than $65,160
Upper-middle-income (3.4–6X poverty)	$31,130–$54,936	$36,924–$65,160
Lower-middle-income (1.85–3.4X poverty)	$16,938–$31,130	$20,091–$36,924
Low-income (< 1.85X poverty)	Less than $16,938	Less than $20,091

Economic Class	Family Size = 4	Family Size = 5
Upper-income (> 6X poverty)	Greater than $83,544	Greater than $98,736
Upper-middle-income (3.4–6X poverty)	$47,341–$83,544	$55,950–$98,736
Lower-middle-income (1.85–3.4X poverty)	$25,759–$47,341	$30,443–$55,950
Low-income (< 1.85X poverty)	Less than $25,759	Less than $30,443

Source: National Center for Education Statistics (2000a) (author calculations).

Appendix B   Logistic Estimates on Earning a Graduate or Professional Degree Within Four Years of Receiving a Bachelor's Degree

Variable	ß	Standard Error	Relative Risk Ratio	T-statistic
Women	.0814	.0925	1.080	0.88
Black	−.2056	.2073	.814	−0.99
Hispanic	.0896	.1979	1.090	0.45
Low-income	−.3137	.1354	.731*	−2.32
Lower-middle-income	−.2232	.1569	.799	−1.42
Upper-middle-income	−.1595	.1334	.853	−1.20
Research/doctoral	.4755	.1249	1.610***	3.81
Comprehensive	.0545	.1375	1.060	0.40
Borrowed as undergraduate	−.0689	.1066	.933	-0.65
Constant	−1.8990	.1648	–	−11.52

Source: National Center for Education Statistics (2000a).
Notes: Weighted N = 684,600
Prob > F, .0003 ***, *** P < .001, * P < .05

Appendix C   Linear Regression Estimates on Total Educational Debt in 1997 Among 1992–1993 College Graduates with an Advanced Degree in 1997

Variables	ß	Standard Error	t-statistic
Women	−5920.729	2025.503	−2.92**
Hispanic	8506.321	6421.875	1.32
African American	−1306.584	3162.944	−0.41
Asian American	576.739	4071.521	0.14
Low-income	−5222.094	2534.396	−2.06*
Lower-middle-income	−5724.534	2678.624	−2.14*
Upper-middle-income	1777.750	2995.652	0.59
Research/doctoral	5314.509	2957.981	1.80
Comprehensive	311.268	3577.039	0.09
Public college	−7345.787	2677.750	−2.74**
Borrowed as undergraduate	18572.670	2273.300	8.17***
Constant	16044.280	2906.221	5.52***

Source: National Center for Education Statistics (2000a).
Notes: Weighted N = 94,561
R^2 = .1636
*** P < .001, ** P < .01, * P < .05

Appendix D **Multinomial Estimates of Educational Debt Burden in 1997 Comparison Group: Debt Burden Declined to Zero Between 1994 and 1997**

Variable	Coefficient	S.E.	RRR	Significance
Women				
Debt burden > 8%	0.0825	0.1147	1.0860	
Debt burden < 8%	−0.1429	0.0948	0.8668	
Hispanic				
Debt burden > 8%	0.3251	0.2539	1.3841	
Debt burden < 8%	0.3313	0.2177	1.3928	
Black				
Debt burden > 8%	0.3676	0.2132	1.4443	~
Debt burden < 8%	0.2983	0.1855	1.3477	~
Asian				
Debt burden > 8%	−0.2419	0.3323	0.7851	
Debt burden < 8%	−0.8258	0.2351	0.4379	***
Low-income				
Debt burden > 8%	1.8880	0.1979	6.6083	***
Debt burden < 8%	1.6598	0.1452	5.2583	***
Lower-middle-income				
Debt burden > 8%	1.0820	0.2125	2.9513	***
Debt burden < 8%	1.0604	0.1579	2.8874	***
Upper-middle-income				
Debt burden > 8%	0.7174	0.1996	2.0489	***
Debt burden < 8%	0.6528	0.1465	1.9209	***
Postgraduate degree in 1997				
Debt burden > 8%	1.0020	0.2596	2.7242	***
Debt burden < 8%	−0.2238	0.2326	0.7995	
Attended public undergraduate institution				
Debt burden > 8%	−0.5733	0.1250	0.5636	***
Debt burden < 8%	−0.2973	0.1045	0.7428	**
BA in business				
Debt burden > 8%	−0.3669	0.2113	0.6928	~
Debt burden < 8%	−0.1802	0.1803	0.8351	
BA in education				
Debt burden > 8%	0.3086	0.2117	1.3616	
Debt burden < 8%	0.0097	0.1715	0.9903	
BA in engineering				
Debt burden > 8%	−0.0623	0.2969	0.9396	
Debt burden < 8%	0.2181	0.2210	1.2438	
BA in health				
Debt burden > 8%	−0.2313	0.2468	0.7935	
Debt burden < 8%	−0.1795	0.1924	0.8357	
BA in social sciences				
Debt burden > 8%	0.1060	0.1921	1.1112	
Debt burden < 8%	−0.3257	0.1623	0.7219	*
BA in biology				
Debt burden > 8%	−0.0528	0.2852	0.9486	
Debt burden < 8%	−0.4028	0.2274	0.6684	~
BA in math				
Debt burden > 8%	−0.1486	0.2554	0.8619	
Debt burden < 8%	−0.3729	0.2035	0.6888	~

Appendix D continues

Appendix D   continued

Variable	Coefficient	S.E.	RRR	Significance
Postgrad social science and humanities				
Debt burden > 8%	−0.0703	0.3289	0.9321	
Debt burden < 8%	−0.0431	0.3113	0.9570	
Postgrad engineering and science				
Debt burden > 8%	−0.8465	0.4566	0.4289	~
Debt burden < 8%	0.0013	0.3848	1.0013	
Postgrad education				
Debt burden > 8%	0.0571	0.3462	1.0587	
Debt burden < 8%	0.7027	0.3117	2.0192	*
Postgrad business and management				
Debt burden > 8%	0.4355	0.4348	1.5457	
Debt burden < 8%	0.6057	0.4262	1.8326	
Postgrad medicine and law				
Debt burden > 8%	−0.0745	0.3266	0.9282	
Debt burden < 8%	0.1284	0.3171	0.8795	
1997 Occupation support services				
Debt burden > 8%	0.1369	0.2153	1.1467	
Debt burden < 8%	−0.0379	0.1738	0.9627	
1997 Occupation professional services				
Debt burden > 8%	0.2292	0.2157	1.2577	
Debt burden < 8%	0.2195	0.1600	1.2455	
1997 Occupation legal				
Debt burden > 8%	0.9069	0.3022	2.4766	**
Debt burden < 8%	0.3942	0.2791	1.4833	
1997 Occupation medical				
Debt burden > 8%	0.5616	0.2427	1.7534	*
Debt burden < 8%	0.4189	0.2017	1.5203	*
1997 Occupation K-12 education				
Debt burden > 8%	0.2629	0.2261	1.3008	
Debt burden < 8%	0.0959	0.1852	1.1007	
1997 Occupation education other				
Debt burden > 8%	0.6819	0.2468	1.9776	**
Debt burden < 8%	−0.1629	0.2186	0.8497	
1997 Occupation professional				
Debt burden > 8%	0.4596	0.2031	1.5834	*
Debt burden < 8%	0.3922	0.1603	1.4802	*
1997 Occupation computer and technical				
Debt burden > 8%	0.2886	0.2395	1.3346	
Debt burden < 8%	0.3381	0.2036	1.4023	~
1997 Occupation management				
Debt burden > 8%	0.0756	0.2258	1.0785	
Debt burden < 8%	0.1733	0.1883	1.1892	
Constant				
Debt burden > 8%	−2.0720	0.2085		***
Debt burden < 8%	−0.8065	0.1965		***

Source: National Center for Education Statistics (2000a).
Notes: Weighted N = 527,286, Prob > F .000 ***, *** P < .001, ** P < .01,
* P < .05, ~ P < .10

Appendix E   Multiple Regression Estimates on 1997 Poverty Index Among 1992–1993 College Graduates

Variables	Unstandardized ß	Standard Error	Significance
Hispanic	−.0347	.1339	*
Black	−.3228	.1585	
Asian	.2469	.2489	
1991 economic class background	.2815	.0326	***
Advanced degree, 1997	−.2658	.1001	**
Married, 1997	1.2950	.0673	***
Research doctoral undergraduate institution	.1535	.0952	
Comprehensive undergraduate institution	.0531	.0992	
Bachelor's degree, business	.4528	.1232	***
Bachelor's degree, education	−.2414	.1035	*
Bachelor's degree, engineering	.9331	.1426	***
Bachelor's degree, health	.8706	.1979	***
Bachelor's degree, social sciences	−.0728	.1079	
Bachelor's degree, biology	−.5788	.1419	***
Bachelor's degree, math	.3297	.1578	*
Constant	2.7467	.1389	

Source: National Center for Education Statistics (2000a).
Notes: Weighted N = 990,908
R^2 = .1220
Prob > F .000 ***, *** $P < .001$, ** $P < .01$, * $P < .05$

References

Advisory Committee on Student Financial Assistance. (2001). *Access Denied: Restoring the Nation's Commitment to Equal Educational Opportunity.* Washington, DC: Advisory Committee on Student Financial Assistance.

————. (2002). *Empty Promises: The Myth of College Access in America.* Washington, DC: Advisory Committee on Student Financial Assistance.

Alliance for Equity in Higher Education. (2003). *Policy Priorities for the Higher Education Act Reauthorization.* Washington, DC: Institute for Higher Education Policy.

American Council on Education. (2002a). *Minorities in Higher Education 2001–2002.* Washington, DC: American Council on Education.

American Council on Education. (2002b). *Attitudes Towards Public Higher Education.* Washington, DC: American Council on Education.

Andersen, M., and P. H. Collins. (1995). *Race, Class, and Gender: An Anthology.* Belmont, CA: Wadsworth.

Archambault, R. D., ed. (1964). *John Dewey on Education, Selected Writing.* New York: Modern Library.

Astin, A., et al. (1996). *Degree Attainment Rates at American Colleges and Universities: Effects of Race, Gender, and Institutional Type.* Los Angeles: Higher Education Research Institute, UCLA.

Baker, M. C. (1966). *Foundations of John Dewey's Educational Theory.* New York: Atherton.

Baum, S., and M. O'Malley. (2003). *College on Credit: How Borrowers Perceive Their Education Debt.* Braintree, MA: Nellie Mae.

Baum, S., and D. Saunders. (1998). *Life After Debt: Results of the National Student Loan Survey.* Braintree, MA: Nellie Mae.

Bergen, M. B., and D. D. Zielke. (1979). "Educational Progress of Basic Educational Opportunity Grant Recipients Compared to Non-recipients." *Journal of Student Financial Aid* 9(1): 19–22.

Blakemore, A. E., and S. A. Low. (1983). "Scholarship Policy and Race-sex Differences in the Demand for Higher Education." *Economic Inquiry* 21: 504–519.

———. (1985). "Public Expenditures on Higher Education and Their Impact on Enrollment Patterns." *Applied Economics* 17: 331–340.

Bowles, S., and H. Gintis. (1976). *Schooling in Capitalist America: Educational Reform and the Contradictions of Economic Life.* New York: Basic Books.

———. (2002). "Schooling in Capitalist America Revisited." *Sociology of Education* 75: 1–18.

Boyd, D. (2002). *State Budget Blues: Western States in the National Context.* Presentation to the annual meeting of the Council of State Governments—WEST. Lake Tahoe, NV, July.

Boyd, J., and C. Wennerdahl. (1993). *The Characteristics of Student Borrowers in Repayment and the Impact of Educational Debt: Summary Report.* Washington, DC: American Council on Education.

Budget of the U.S. Government, Fiscal Year 2003. Washington, DC: Government Printing Office. Available online at www.access.gpo.gov/usbudget/fy2003/pdf/budget.pdf.

Carnoy, M. (1974). *Education as Cultural Imperialism.* New York: David McKay.

———. (1993). "School Improvement: Is Privatization the Answer?" In *Decentralization and School Improvement.* Eds. Jane Hannaway and Martin Carnoy. San Francisco: Jossey-Bass.

Chow, E. N. (1996). "Introduction: Transforming Knowledge-ment—Race, Class, and Gender." In *Race, Class, and Gender: Common Bonds, Different Voices.* Eds. Esther Ngan-

Ling Chow, Doris Wilkinson, and Maxine Baca Zinn. Thousand Oaks, CA: Sage.

Choy, S. P. (2002). *Access and Persistence: Findings from 10 Years of Longitudinal Research on Students.* Washington, DC: American Council on Education.

Clarke, D. L., and T. A. Astuto. (1990). "The Disjunction of Federal Educational Policy and National Educational Needs in the 1990s." In *Education Politics for the New Century*. Eds. Douglas E. Mitchell and Margaret E. Goertz. London: Falmer.

Cofer, J., and P. Somers. (1999). "An Analytical Approach to Understanding Student Debtload Response." *Journal of Student Financial Aid* 29(3): 25–44.

———. (2000). "A Comparison of the Influence of Debtload on the Persistence of Students at Public and Private Colleges." *Journal of Student Financial Aid* 30(2): 39–58.

College Board. (2002a). *Trends in College Pricing, 2002.* New York: College Board.

———. (2002b). *Trends in Student Aid, 2002.* New York: College Board.

Collins, P. H. (1991). *Black Feminist Thought: Knowledge, Consciousness, and the Politics of Empowerment.* New York: Routledge.

———. (1998). "On Book Exhibits and New Complexities: Reflections on Sociology as Science." *Contemporary Sociology* 27(1): 7–11.

Collins, R. (1979). *The Credential Society: An Historical Sociology of Education and Stratification.* New York: Academic Press.

Cox, O. C. (1948). *Caste, Class, and Race: A Study in Social Dynamics.* New York: Doubleday.

Davis, J. S. (1997). *College Affordability: A Closer Look at the Crisis.* Reston, VA: Sallie Mae Education Institute.

———. (2003). *Unintended Consequences of Tuition-Discounting.* Indianapolis, IN: Lumina Foundation for Education, New Agenda Series.

Davis, J. S., and K. Johns Jr. (1989). "Changes in Low-income Freshmen Participation in College, 1966 to 1986." *Journal of Student Financial Aid* 19(1): 56–62.

Davis, J. S., and J. K. Wohlford. (2001). "Enrollment Characteristics of College Freshmen." Unpublished manuscript. Indianapolis, IN: Lumina Foundation for Education.

Dewey, J. (1916). *Democracy and Education: An Introduction to the Philosophy of Education.* New York: Macmillan.

Duncan, G. J. (1994). "Families and Neighbors as Sources of Disadvantage in the Schooling Decisions of White and Black Adolescents." *American Journal of Education* 103 (November): 20–53.

ECMC Group Foundation. (2003). *Cultural Barriers to Incurring Debt: An Exploration of Borrowing and Impact on Access to Postsecondary Education.* Prepared by Caliber Associates. Santa Fe, NM: ECMC Group Foundation.

Feagin, J. R., and H. Vera. (1995). *White Racism.* New York: Routledge.

Fuller, R., and R. Schoenberger. (1991). "The Gender Salary Gap: Do Academic Achievement, Internship Experience, and College Major Make a Difference?" *Social Science Quarterly* 72(4): 715–726.

Galloway, F. J. (1994). *The Importance of High School Related Skills in the Primary and Secondary Labor Markets.* Unpublished diss., Graduate School of Education, Harvard University.

Ganzeboom, H. B. G., D. J. Treiman, and W. C. Ulte. (1991). "Comparative Intergenerational Stratification Research." *Annual Review of Sociology* 17: 277–302.

Geiger, R. (1999). "The Ten Generations of American Higher Education." In *American Higher Education in the Twenty-First Century.* Eds. P. G. Altbach, R. O. Berdahl, and P. J. Gumport. Baltimore: Johns Hopkins University Press.

Gittleman, M. B., and D. R. Howell. (1995). "Changes in the Structure and Quality of Jobs in the United States: Effects of Race and Gender, 1973–1990." *Industrial and Labor Relations Review* 48(3): 420–440.

Goyette, K., and Y. Xie. (1999). "Educational Expectations of Asian American Youths: Determinants and Ethnic Differences." *Sociology of Education* 72(1): 22–36.

Green, P. J., et al. (1996). *Baccalaureate and Beyond Longitudinal Study: 1993/94 First Follow-Up Methodology Report.* NCES 96–149. Washington, DC: U.S. Department of Education, National Center for Education Statistics.

Green, P. J., et al. (1999). *Baccalaureate and Beyond Longitudinal*

Study: 1993/97 Second Follow-Up Methodology Report. NCES 99–159. Washington, DC: U.S. Department of Education, National Center for Education Statistics.

Gutman, A. (1998). "Undemocratic Education." In *Philosophy of Education: Major Themes in the Analytic Tradition, Volume 3: Society and Education.* Eds. P. H. Hirst and P. White. New York: Routledge.

Hansen, W. L., and J. O. Stampen. (1994). "Economics and Financing Higher Education: The Tension Between Quality and Equity." In *Higher Education in American Society*, 3rd ed. Eds., Philip G. Altbach, Robert O. Berdahl, and Patricia J. Gumport. Amherst, NY: Prometheus Books.

Hauptman, A. M. (2001). "Reforming the Ways in Which States Finance Higher Education." In *The States and Public Higher Education Policy.* Ed. D. E. Heller. Baltimore: Johns Hopkins University Press.

Hearn, J. C. (1990). "Pathways to Attendance at the Elite Colleges." In *The High Status Track: Studies of Elite Schools and Stratification.* Eds. Paul William Kingston and Lionel S. Lewis. Albany: State University of New York Press.

————. (1993). "The Paradox of Growth in Federal Aid for College Students, 1965–1990." In *Higher Education: Handbook of Theory and Research*, vol. 9. Ed. John C. Smart. New York: Agathon.

Heller, D. E. (1996). "Tuition, Financial Aid, and Access to Public Higher Education." Unpublished diss. Cambridge, MA: Harvard University, Graduate School of Education.

————. (1997). Student Price Response in Higher Education: An Update to Leslie and Brinkman. *Journal of Higher Education* 68(6): 624–659.

————. (1999). "The Effects of Tuition and State Financial Aid on Public College Enrollment." *Review of Higher Education* 23 (1): 65–89.

————. (2001a). *Debts and Decisions: Student Loans and Their Relationship to Graduate School and Career Choice.* Indianapolis, IN: Lumina Foundation for Education, New Agenda Series.

————. (2001b). *The States and Public Higher Education Policy: Affordability, Access, and Accountability.* Baltimore: Johns Hopkins University Press.

Hertz, T. (2001). *Intergenerational Transition Probabilities in the*

PSID. Princeton, NJ: Princeton University, Center for Health and Well-being.

Howe, K. R. (1998). "In Defense of Outcomes-based Conceptions of Equal Educational Opportunity." In *Philosophy of Education: Major Themes in the Analytic Tradition, Volume 3: Society and Education*. Eds. P. H. Hirst and P. White. New York: Routledge.

Institute for Higher Education Policy. (1998). *Do Grants Matter? Student Grant Aid and College Affordability*. Washington, DC: Institute for Higher Education Policy.

Institute for Higher Education Policy, and The Education Resources Institute. (1995). *College Debt and the American Family*. Washington, DC: The Institute for Higher Education Policy.

Jackson, G. A. (1978). "Financial Aid and Student Enrollment." *Journal of Higher Education* 49 (6): 548–574.

Jacobs, J. A. (1996). "Gender Inequality and Higher Education." *Annual Review of Sociology* 22: 153–185.

Kane, T. J. (1999). *The Price of Admission: Rethinking How Americans Pay for College*. Washington, DC: Brookings Institution Press.

Karen, D. (2002). "Changes in Access to Higher Education in the United States: 1980–1992." *Sociology of Education* 75: 191–210.

King, D. (1988). "Multiple Jeopardy, Multiple Consciousness: The Context of a Black Feminist Ideology." *Signs: Journal of Women in Culture and Society* 14: 42–72.

King, J. E. (1996). "Student Aid: Who Benefits Now?" *Educational Record* (Winter): 21–27.

King, T., and E. Bannon. (2002). *The Burden of Borrowing: A Report on the Rising Rates of Student Loan Debt*. Washington, DC: State PIRG's Higher Education Project.

Kingston, P., and J. C. Smart. (1990). "The Economic Pay-off of Prestigious Colleges." In *The High Status Track: Studies of Elite Schools and Stratification*. Eds. Paul William Kingston and Lionel S. Lewis. Albany: State University of New York Press.

Kipp, S., D. V. Price, and J. K. Wohlford. (2002). *Unequal Opportunities: Disparities in College Access Across the Fifty States*. Indianapolis, IN: Lumina Foundation for Education, New Agenda Series.

Labaree, D. F. (1997). *How to Succeed in School Without Really*

Learning: The Credentials Race in American Education. New Haven, CT: Yale University Press.

Leslie, L. L., and P. T. Brinkman. (1987). "Student Price Response in Higher Education." *Journal of Higher Education* 58 (2): 181–204.

Long, J. S. (1997). *Regression Models for Categorical and Limited Dependent Variables.* Thousand Oaks, CA: Sage.

Lumina Foundation for Education. (2002). *Higher Education, Increasingly Important for All Americans, Is Unaffordable for Many.* Indianapolis, IN: Lumina Foundation for Education, Illuminations.

———. (2003a). *Enrollments in Postsecondary Education for Pell Grant Recipients.* Unpublished data. Indianapolis, IN: Lumina Foundation for Education.

———. (2003b). *Predicting Student Success at Four-Year Colleges.* Unpublished Data. Indianapolis, IN: Lumina Foundation for Education.

Manski, C. F., and D. A. Wise. (1983). *College Choice in America.* Cambridge, MA: Harvard University Press.

MATHTECH Inc. (1998). *Factors Related to College Enrollment, Final Report.* Washington, DC: Advisory Committee on Student Financial Assistance. Available online at www.ed. gov/offices/OUS/PES/finaid/enroll98.pdf.

McCarthy, C., and W. Crichlow. (1993). "Introduction: Theories of Identity, Theories of Representation, Theories of Race." In *Race, Identity, and Representation in Education.* Eds. Cameron McCarthy and Warren Crichlow. New York: Routledge.

McCreight, K., and M. LeMay. (1982). "A Longitudinal Study of the Achievement and Persistence of Students Who Received Basic Educational Opportunity Grants." *Journal of Student Financial Aid* 12(1): 11–15.

McKeown-Moak, M. P. (1999). *Financing Higher Education: An Annual Report from the States, 1999.* Tallahassee, FL: State Higher Education Executive Officers Association.

McPherson, M., and M. O. Schapiro. (1998). *The Student Aid Game: Meeting Need and Rewarding Talent in Higher Education.* Princeton, NJ: Princeton University Press.

Millett, C. M. (2003). "How Undergraduate Loan Debt Affects Application and Enrollment in Graduate or First Professional School." *Journal of Higher Education* 74 (4): 386–427.

Mortenson, T. G. (1998). "How Will We Do More With Less: The Public Policy Dilemma of Financing Postsecondary Educational Opportunity." In *Condemning Students to Debt: College Loans and Public Policy*. Eds. R. Fossey and M. Bateman. New York: Teachers College Press.

Mumper, M. (1996). *Removing College Price Barriers: What Government Has Done and Why It Hasn't Worked*. Albany: State University of New York Press.

———. (2001). "State Efforts to Keep Public Colleges Affordable in the Face of Fiscal Stress." In *The Finance of Higher Education: Theory, Research, Policy, and Practice*. Eds. M. B. Paulsen and J. C. Smart. New York: Agathon.

Murdock, T. A. (1987). "It Isn't Just Money: The Effects of Financial Aid on Student Persistence." *Review of Higher Education* 11(1): 75–101.

National Association of State Student Grant and Aid Programs. (2003). *33rd Annual Survey Report on State-Sponsored Student Financial Aid, 2001–2002 Academic Year*. Prepared by K. DeSalvatore, L. Hughes, and E. Gee. New York: New York State Higher Education Services Corporation.

National Center for Education Statistics (U.S. Department of Education). (1998a). *Access to Postsecondary Education for the 1992 High School Graduates*. By L. Berkner and L. Chavez. Washington, DC: National Center for Education Statistics.

———. (1998b). *Inequalities in Public School District Revenues*. Washington, DC: National Center for Education Statistics.

———. (2000a). *Baccalaureate and Beyond Longitudinal Survey: 93/97*. Washington, DC: U.S. Department of Education, National Center for Education Statistics.

———. (2000b). *The Condition of Education*. Washington, DC: National Center for Education Statistics.

———. (2000c). *Debt Burden Four Years After College*. By S. Choy. NCES 2000188. Washington, DC: National Center for Education Statistics.

———. (2001a). *The Condition of Education*. Washington, DC: National Center for Education Statistics.

———. (2001c). *Educational Achievement and Black-White Inequality*. By J. Jacobson, et al. Washington, DC: National Center for Education Statistics.

———. (2001d). *Study of College Costs and Prices, 1988–89 to*

1997–98, vol. 1. By A. F. Cunningham, et al. Washington, DC: National Center for Education Statistics.

———. (2002a). *Digest of Education Statistics, 2001.* Washington, DC: National Center for Education Statistics.

———. (2002b). *Student Financing of Undergraduate Education: 1999–2000.* Washington, DC: National Center for Education Statistics.

———. (2002c). *What Students Pay for College: Changes in Net Price of College Attendance Between 1992–93 and 1999–2000.* By L. Horn, C. C. Wei, and A. Berker. Washington, DC: National Center for Education Statistics.

———. (2003a). *Characteristics of Undergraduate Borrowers, 1999–2000.* By M. E. Clinedinst, A. F. Cunningham, and J. P. Merisotis. Washington, DC: National Center for Education Statistics.

———. (2003b). *Digest of Education Statistics, 2002.* Washington, DC: National Center for Education Statistics.

National Center for Public Policy and Higher Education. (2002). *Losing Ground: A National Status Report on the Affordability of American Higher Education.* San Jose, CA: National Center for Public Policy and Higher Education.

National Commission on Responsibilities for Financing Postsecondary Education. (1993). *Making College Affordable Again.* Washington, DC: National Commission on Responsibilities for Financing Postsecondary Education.

Nussbaum, M. C. (1997). *Cultivating Humanity: A Classical Defense of Reform in Liberal Education.* Cambridge, MA: Harvard University Press.

Oliver, M. L., and T. M. Shapiro. (1995). *Black Wealth/White Wealth.* London: Routledge.

Perna, L. W. (1998). "The Contribution of Financial Aid to Undergraduate Persistence." *Journal of Student Financial Aid* 28(3): 25–40.

Perna, L. W., and M. A. Titus. (2002). *Understanding Differences in the Choice of College Attended: The Role of State Context.* Paper presented to Public Policy Pre-Conference, Association for the Study of Higher Education, Sacramento, CA, November.

Persell, C. H., S. Catsambis, and P. W. Cookson Jr. (1992). "Differential Asset Conversion: Class and Gendered Pathways to Selective Colleges." *Sociology of Education* 65: 208–225.

Price, D. V. (1999). "Systems of Inequality: Student Indebtedness and Early Labor Market Incorporation." Diss. Washington, DC: American University. Available at UMI Dissertation Services (99440000), www.umi.com.

———. (Forthcoming). "Educational Debt Burden Among Student Borrowers: An Analysis of the Baccalaureate and Beyond Panel, 1997 Follow-up." *Research in Higher Education* 45 (7), November 2004.

Ravitch, D. (2001). "Education and Democracy." In *Making Good Citizens: Education and Civil Society.* Eds. D. Ravitch and J. P. Viteretti. New Haven, CT: Yale University Press.

Reed, A. Jr. (2001). "A GI Bill for Everybody." Dissent 48 (4). Available online at www.djdinstitute.org.

Reischauer, R. D. (1993). "Apply the Social Insurance Concept to Student Loans." In *Radical Reform or Incremental Change: Student Loan Policy Alternatives for the Federal Government.* Ed. L. E. Gladieux. New York: College Board.

Scherschel, P. M. (1998). *Student Indebtedness: Are Borrowers Pushing the Limits?* Indianapolis, IN: USA Group Foundation.

———. (2000). *Student Debt Levels Continue to Rise: Stafford Indebtedness, 1999 Update.* Indianapolis, IN: USA Group Foundation.

Schrag, P. G. (2002). *Repay as You Earn: The Flawed Government Program to Help Students Have Public Service Careers.* Westport, CT: Bergin and Garvey.

Schwartz, J. B. (1985). "Student Financial Aid and the College Enrollment Decision: The Effects of Public and Private Grants and Interest Subsidies." *Economics of Education Review 4* (2), 129–144.

Slamming Shut the Doors to College: The State Budget Crisis and Higher Education. (2002). Congressional report prepared by the Democratic Staffs of Senators Kennedy, Harkin, and Reid and Representatives Miller and Obey. Washington, DC. Available online at edworkforce.house.gov/democrats/higheredreport.pdf (accessed September 26, 2002).

Spilerman, S., N. Lewin-Epstein, and M. Semyonov. (1993). "Wealth, Intergenerational Transfers, and Life Chances." In *Social Theory and Social Policy: Essays in Honor of James S. Coleman.* Eds. Aage B. Sorensen and Seymour Spilerman. Westport, CT: Praeger.

St. John, E. P. (1989). "The Influence of Student Aid on Persistence." *Journal of Student Financial Aid* 19(3): 52–68.

———. (1990). "Price Response in Enrollment Decisions: An Analysis of the High School and Beyond Sophomore Cohort." *Research in Higher Education* 31(2): 161–176.

———. (1991). "The Impact of Student Financial Aid: A Review of Recent Research." *Journal of Student Financial Aid* 21(1): 18–32.

———. (2002). *The Access Challenge: Rethinking the New Inequality.* Bloomington: Indiana Education Policy Center.

———. (2003). *Refinancing the College Dream: Access, Equal Opportunity, and Justice for Taxpayers.* Baltimore: Johns Hopkins University Press.

St. John, E. P., and R. J. Eliot. (1994). "Reframing Policy Research: A Critical Examination of Research on Federal Student Aid Programs." In *Higher Education: Handbook of Theory and Research,* vol. 10. Ed. J. C. Smart. New York: Agathon.

St. John, E. P., et al. (2002). *Meeting the Access Challenge: Indiana's Twenty-First Century Scholars Program.* Indianapolis, IN: Lumina Foundation for Education, New Agenda Series.

Stiglitz, J. E., et al. (2000). *The Impact of Paying for College on Family Finances.* Sebago Associates, Inc., November. Available online at www.sbgo.com.

Szymanski, S. (2002). *Free Tuition at All Public Colleges and Universities for Students Who Meet Admission Standards.* Washington, DC: The Debs Jones Douglass Institute.

Terkla, D. G. (1985). "Does Financial Aid Enhance Undergraduate Persistence?" *Journal of Student Financial Aid* 15(3): 11–18.

Thomas, R. S. (1998). *Black and Latino College Enrollment: Effects of Background, High School Preparation, Family and Peer Influence, and Financial Aid.* Paper presented at the annual meeting of the American Educational Research Association, San Diego, California.

Thomas, S. L. (2003). "Longer-term Economic Effects of College Selectivity and Control." *Research in Higher Education* 44(3): 263–299.

Thomas, S. L., and R. H. Heck. (2001). "Analysis of Large-scale Secondary Data in Higher Education Research: Potential Perils Associated with Complex Sampling Designs." *Research in Higher Education* 42(5): 517–540.

Thomas, S. L., and L. Zhang. (2001). *Post-baccalaureate Wage Growth Within Four Years of Graduation: The Effects of College Major, Quality, and Performance.* Paper presented to the annual meeting of the Association for the Study of Higher Education, Richmond, Virginia.

Ulrich, R. (1970) *Fundamentals of Democratic Education: An Introduction to Educational Philosophy.* Westport, CT: Greenwood.

U.S. Bureau of the Census. (2002). *Current Population Survey, March 2002.* Washington, DC: U.S. Census Bureau.

———. (2003). *Percent of People 25 Years Old and Over Who Have Completed High School or College by Race, Hispanic Origin and Sex: Selected Years 1940–2002.* Washington, DC: U.S. Census Bureau. Available online at www.census.gov/population/socdemo/education/tabA-2.pdf.

Useem, M. (1989). *Liberal Education and the Corporation.* New York: Aldine de Gruyter.

Useem, M., and J. Karabel. (1990). Pathways to Top Corporate Management. In *The High Status Track: Studies of Elite Schools and Stratification.* Eds. Paul William Kingston and Lionel S. Lewis. Albany: State University of New York Press.

U.S. General Accounting Office. (2003). *Student Financial Aid: Monitoring Aid Greater Than Federally Defined Need Could Help Address Student Loan Indebtedness* (GAO-03-508). Washington, DC: U.S. Government Accounting Office.

Veblen, T. (1918). *The Higher Learning in America.* New York: Sentry.

Wagoner, J. L. Jr. (1976) *Thomas Jefferson and the Education of a New Nation.* Bloomington, IN: Phi Delta Kappa Educational Foundation.

West, C. (1997). "Afterword." In *The House That Race Built.* Ed. Wahneema Lubiano. New York: Pantheon.

West, C., and S. Fenstermaker. (1996). "Doing Difference." In *Race, Class, and Gender: Common Bonds, Different Voices.* Eds. Esther Ngan-Ling Chow, Doris Wilkinson, and Maxine Baca Zinn. Thousand Oaks, CA: Sage.

Wilson, K. L., and J. P. Boldizar. (1990). "Gender Segregation in Higher Education: Effects of Aspiration, Mathematics Achievement, and Income." *Sociology of Education* 63 (January): 62–74.

Wright, E. O. (1985). *Classes*. London: New Left Books.

———. (1997). *Class Counts*. Cambridge, UK: Cambridge University Press.

Young, G., and B. J. Dickerson, eds. (1994). *Color, Class, and Country: Experiences of Gender*. London: Zed Books.

Zumeta, W. (2001). "Public Policy and Accountability in Higher Education: Lessons Learned from the Past and Present for the New Millennium." In *The States and Public Higher Education Policy*. Ed. D. E. Heller. Baltimore: Johns Hopkins University Press.

Index

About the Book

A s the cost of higher education continues to rise, students increasingly rely on borrowing to pay for college. But is the result the improved socioeconomic position that they anticipate? *Borrowing Inequality* explores the real impact of loans on minority and low-income students.

Drawing on a national study of student borrowing patterns, Derek Price finds that racial and ethnic minorities and low-income students are not only more likely to borrow than their white and upper-income peers, they also are less likely to graduate from high-status institutions and go on to graduate school. In addition, current loan programs can burden student borrowers in that their career opportunities are restricted, in effect perpetuating the very patterns of inequality that the programs were intended to alleviate. While the graduates' prospects clearly are higher than they would have been without higher education, the structural pattern of inequality continues to reflect race, ethnic, gender, and class characteristics.

Price concludes with provocative proposals for aid policies that would expand the range of college and career choices for students—policies that would in fact support the role of higher education as a vehicle for individual opportunity and social change.

Derek V. Price is the director of higher education research at the Lumina Foundation for Education. The views and opinions expressed are exclusively those of the author and are not necessarily those of the Lumina Foundation for Education, Inc.